~~~ **VOLUME 2** ~~~

Under the Sea Lessons for Life

Teacher + Counselor Activity Guide

Integrating social-emotional
growth and academic development

Grades K-5

Boys Town, Nebraska

Illustrated by **BRIAN MARTIN** Written by **SARA KINSEY**

Under the Sea Lessons for Life: Teacher + Counselor Activity Guide Volume 2
Text and Illustrations Copyright © 2025 by Father Flanagan's Boys' Home
ISBN: 979-8-88907-035-1

Published by Boys Town Press, 13603 Flanagan Blvd., Boys Town, Nebraska 68010

All rights reserved under International and Pan-American Copyright Conventions. Unless otherwise noted, no part of this book may be reproduced, stored in a retrieval system, or transmitted in any form or by any means, electronic, mechanical, photocopying, recording or otherwise, without express written permission of the publisher, except for brief quotations or critical reviews. The activity sheets are available for download and may be reproduced without special permission for use in individual classrooms.

For a Boys Town Press catalog, call 1-800-282-6657 or visit our website: BoysTownPress.org

Publisher's Cataloging-in-Publication Data

Names: Kinsey, Sara (Sara Elizabeth), author | Martin, Brian (Brian Michael), 1978- illustrator.

Title: Under the sea lessons for life. Volume 2, Teacher + counselor activity guide : integrating social-emotional growth and academic development / written by Sara Kinsey ; illustrated by Brian Martin.

Identifiers: ISBN: 979-8-88907-035-1

Subjects: LCSH: Success in children--Study and teaching. | Social learning--Study and teaching. | Emotional intelligence--Study and teaching. | Emotions in children--Study and teaching. | Self-control in children--Study and teaching. | Academic achievement--Study and teaching. | Personality and academic achievement--Study and teaching. | Motivation in education--Study and teaching. | Life skills--Study and teaching. | Social skills--Study and teaching. | Children--Life skills guides--Study and teaching. | BISAC: EDUCATION / Counseling / Academic Development. | EDUCATION / Decision-Making & Problem Solving. | EDUCATION / Counseling/Crisis Management. | EDUCATION / Educational Psychology.

Classification: LCC: BF723.S77 K56 2025 | DDC: 155.4/19--dc23

Printed in the United States
10 9 8 7 6 5 4 3 2 1

Boys Town Press is the publishing division of Boys Town, a national organization serving children and families.

Instructions to download worksheets, handouts, and student storybook

ACCESS:
boystownpress.org/book-downloads

ENTER:
Your first and last names
Email address
Code: **888907uts0351**
Check yes to receive emails to ensure your email link is received.

TABLE OF CONTENTS

SEL STORIES FROM UNDER THE SEA
Welcome and Introduction.. v-vi

FRODO MANDARIN FISH.............................. 1
  Story...2-3
  Activities.................................... 4-26

SHAKTI EPAULETTE SHARK 27
  Story... 28-29
  Activities....................................30-52

NIKO NUDIBRANCH 53
  Story... 54-55
  Activities....................................56-76

SEABORN BRITTLE STAR 77
  Story... 78-79
  Activities.................................... 80-102

KACIE DISCO CLAM................................ 103
  Story...104-105
  Activities................................... 106-124

ANSWER KEYS 125-127
TIPS 128-130
GLOSSARY... 131

NOTE: SOME ACADEMIC LESSONS MAY REQUIRE MORE SUPPORT AND ADAPTATION FOR EARLY-ELEMENTARY STUDENTS.

Teacher + Counselor Activity Guide

SEL Stories from Under the Sea

**WELCOME TO THE UNDERWATER WORLD OF THE RAJA AMPAT REEF,
HOME TO AN AMAZING ARRAY OF SEA CREATURES AND MARINE LIFE!**

This vibrant ecosystem located in the western Pacific Ocean, off the coast of Indonesia, is teeming with diversity, color, and wonder. It is symbolic of the classrooms and learning environments we want all our children to inhabit. The reef and the sea life it nourishes are the inspiration for this collection of short stories and supporting activities.

Five tales, written in rhyme, highlight the life-long benefits children can enjoy when they develop and strengthen their social and emotional skills. With the help of lovable and relatable characters – Frodo Mandarin Fish, Shakti Epaulette Shark, Niko Nudibranch, Seaborn Brittle Star, and Kacie Disco Clam – the following skills are brought to life: **self-confidence, accountability, problem solving, compromising,** and **self-control.**

How to Use the Activity Guide

Each skill is introduced in a story written to capture a child's attention and then supplemented by fun, engaging activities that support further skill development and academic growth. The activities allow children to explore art, movement, science and technology, writing, math, music, coloring, and structured group discussion.

You can blend the activities into existing academic lesson plans or subject areas, assign as homework, or teach as stand-alone lessons. Every activity features a list of materials, step-by-step teacher instructions, and any necessary supporting materials, such as worksheets and handouts.

The activities can be individualized or modified to accommodate the needs, capabilities, and learning styles of your students. The variety of options allows you to pick and choose multiple ways to help students enhance their understanding of a skill while growing academically. Some activities are specifically designed for collaboration and group work, while others can be done independently.

Storybook and Support Material PDFs

For your classroom, you can download a printable, full-color PDF student version of *Under the Sea*. All five stories, plus color photos and illustrations of the animals, are included, along with a helpful glossary highlighting words that may be new or unfamiliar to K-5 students. At the end of each story, a fun trivia question will test their knowledge about the marine animal. You can access PDFs of the storybook and additional support materials using the special code listed on the inside front cover of this guide.

Promote Life Skills and Academic Growth

The stories combined with the activities focus on the development of the whole child and the social skills they need for greater success in school, in their relationships, and in life! As children acquire and improve their understanding and use of social skills, you can expect to see greater confidence, improved problem solving and decision making, more flexible thinking, and, best of all, engaged learners and empowered individuals.

As an added benefit, this material offers you an opportunity to introduce academic lessons or discussions about other important and timely topics, such as biodiversity, endangered species, marine ecosystems, or the impacts of climate change.

Two-Volume Series

This is Volume Two in a two-volume series. Volume One featured the skills of managing stress, using whole-body listening, resolving conflicts, expressing empathy, and making friends. The skills were explained with the help of animals that included a dugong, a bottlenose dolphin, a blue-ringed octopus, a manta ray, and a hawksbill sea turtle. Used together, Volumes One and Two offer foundational skills that will help K-5 students find success in and out of the classroom.

MANDARIN FISH

SKILL — FRODO, A MANDARIN FISH, USED TO BULLY OTHERS. HE WAS VERY CONTROLLING AND WOULD TRY TO GET NUDIBRANCH TO JOIN IN THE BULLYING. HE WAS VERY INSECURE AND DIDN'T LIKE THAT HE WAS DIFFERENT FROM OTHER FISH, UNTIL HE LEARNED ABOUT SELF-CONFIDENCE FROM THE EPAULETTE SHARK. AFTER THAT, FRODO REALIZED IT'S OKAY TO BE DIFFERENT. NOW, HE GOES AROUND TEACHING THE IMPORTANCE OF DIVERSITY AND ACCEPTANCE.

MANDARIN FISH
Self-Confidence, Diversity, and Acceptance

The name Frodo means enlightened by life's experiences.

*Frodo Fish and Ollie Octopus were always partners in crime.
Doing stuff together is how they spent all of their time.*

*The two were bullies to the other creatures in the sea.
They wanted another pal to make them a group of three.*

*They threatened Niko until he cried,
because they wanted him by their side.*

*They said if he didn't help pick on kids,
they would feed him to the hungry squids.*

*Niko reported it to the teachers.
They were disappointed with the creatures.*

*Frodo thought picking on others would make him cool,
but being a bully is really, really cruel.*

*Being mean is never okay.
It makes other creatures feel gray.*

*The teacher tried to find out why-oh-why
Frodo Fish would make others cry.*

*Frodo picked on any sea creature who looked weak,
because he was insecure about being unique.*

*Frodo does not have fish scales,
but he does have colorful details.*

*Frodo's colors always shine bright.
He is a beautiful sight.*

Frodo is jealous of the other fish.
Having scales is his one and only wish.

Frodo's teacher sent him to talk to Shakti Shark,
so Shakti could give Frodo a self-confidence spark.

Frodo was inspired by his new shark friend.
He promised his mean days were at an end.

Frodo Fish learned that looks do not matter,
but your personality will cause chatter.

Others will not want to be around you if you are mean.
You need to treat them with respect if you want to be seen.

Being a bully will make others want to run and hide,
but if you treat them with kindness, they will stand by your side.

A true friend will not care how you look or if you are smart.
A friend will only care about what they see in your heart.

If everyone looked the same,
the world would be rather lame.

Being different colors and sizes
is one of the ocean's greatest prizes.

We are all different inside and out,
but acceptance is what it's all about.

Q: Mandarin fish are sometimes referred to as this: moon fish / spilled paint fish / psychedelic fish / electric blue fish

A: Psychedelic Fish

We should give our differences more appreciation
and continue our diversity education.

Learning about differences helps us better understand
why others are the way they are and how to work together hand in hand.

Always celebrate the creature you are.
As long as you are kind, you're a shining star.

Mandarin Fish Poster

MATERIALS

- Oil Pastels/Colored Pencils/Crayons/Markers
- Drawing Paper/Poster Board
- "Mandarin Fish" poster

TEACHER INSTRUCTIONS

1. Distribute the "Mandarin Fish" drawing paper.

2. Instruct students to recreate the image of a Mandarin fish, using oil pastels or other coloring tools.

3. Ask for volunteers to show their drawings, then discuss what makes each drawing unique.

Teacher + Counselor Activity Guide

Name: _____   Date: _____

Mandarin Fish Poster

DIRECTIONS: Draw and color a picture of a Mandarin fish. Be prepared to show your drawing and discuss what makes it unique.

Under the Sea Lessons for Life – Volume 2

Frodo Mandarin Fish Discussion Questions

MATERIALS

- Pencils
- "Discussion Questions" worksheet

TEACHER INSTRUCTIONS

1. Pass out the "Discussion Questions" worksheet.
2. Instruct students to fill out the worksheet by answering the questions.
3. Read the questions aloud and discuss possible answers as a group.
4. Optional: As a class, read *Ollie Octopus,* a story about conflict resolution, from Volume 1 of *Under the Sea: Lessons for Life.*

CLASS/GROUP DISCUSSION QUESTIONS

1. What does it mean to report?
2. How is reporting different from tattling or snitching?
3. What are examples of things that should be reported?
4. Is it ever okay to be mean to someone?
5. What should you do if someone asks you to say or do mean things to others?
6. How do you think most bullies really feel inside?
7. What does it mean to have self-confidence?
8. Why is it important to celebrate our differences?

Teacher + Counselor Activity Guide

Name: _____ Date: _____

Discussion Questions

DIRECTIONS: In the space provided, answer the following questions. Be prepared to discuss your answers with the group.

1. What does it mean to report? _____
   _____
   _____
   _____
   _____

2. How is reporting different from tattling or snitching? _____
   _____
   _____
   _____
   _____

3. What are examples of things that should be reported? _____
   _____
   _____
   _____
   _____

4. Is it ever okay to be mean to someone? _____
   _____
   _____
   _____
   _____

Discussion Questions continued

5. What should you do if someone asks you to say or do mean things to others? _____
   _____
   _____
   _____
   _____

6. How do you think most bullies really feel inside? _____
   _____
   _____
   _____
   _____

7. What does it mean to have self-confidence? _____
   _____
   _____
   _____
   _____

8. Why is it important to celebrate our differences? _____
   _____
   _____
   _____
   _____

Drawing Activity

MATERIALS

- Colored Pencils/Crayons/Markers
- "I'm Unique and Distinct" Paper/Poster Board

TEACHER INSTRUCTIONS

1. Distribute the "I'm Unique and Distinct" paper/poster board.
2. Review with students the directions for the poster.
3. Ask for volunteers to show and explain their drawings.

Name: _____ Date: _____

I'm Unique and Distinct Poster

DIRECTIONS: Draw a picture that features all the things that make you unique.

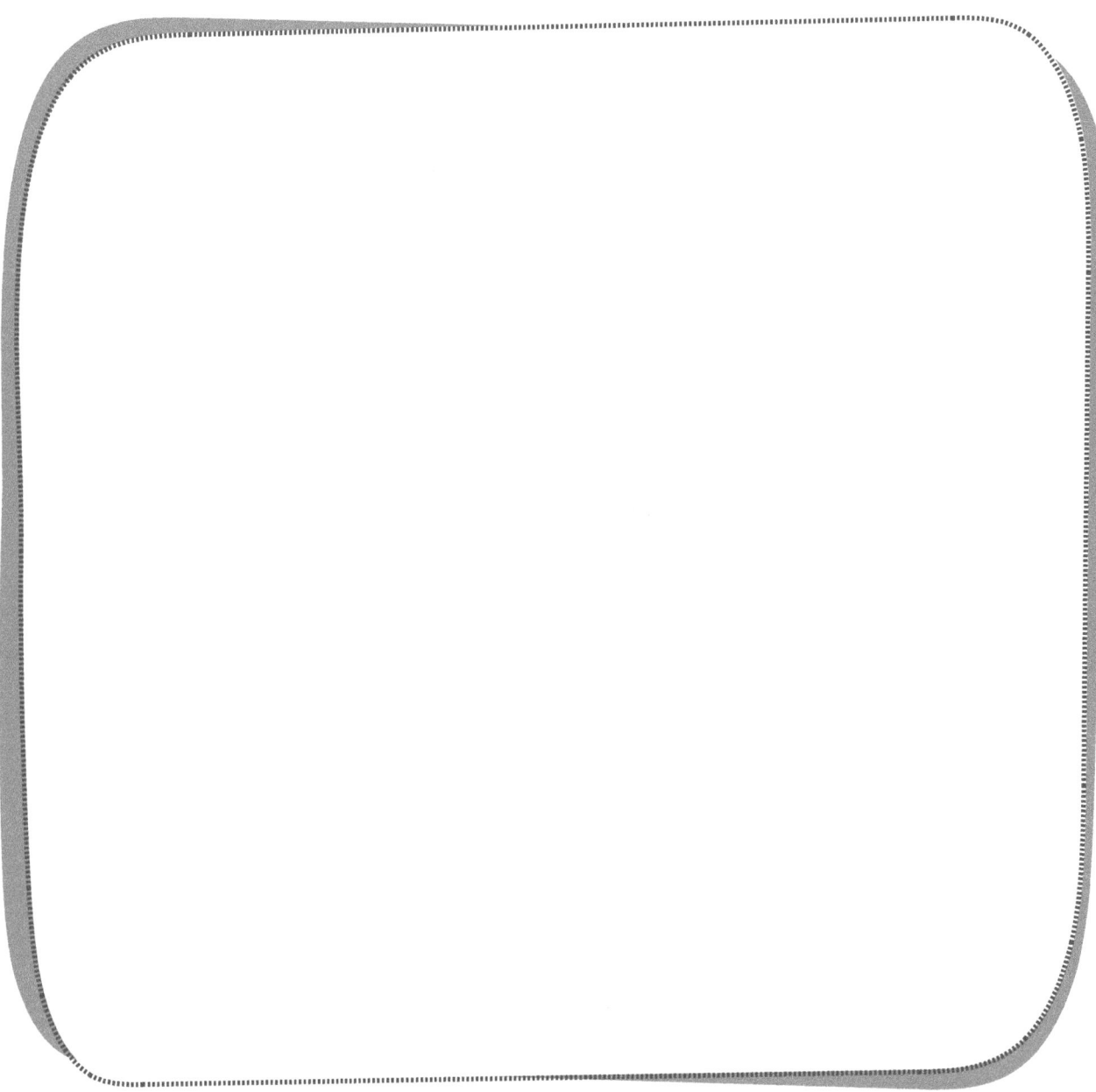

Fish and Sharks

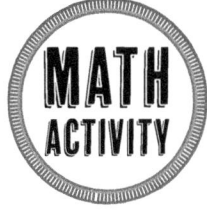

MATERIALS

- "Fish and Sharks" worksheet
- Several pictures of different species of fish
- Several pictures of different species of sharks

TEACHER INSTRUCTIONS

1. Give each student (or group) pictures of fish and sharks.

2. Instruct the students (or groups) to sort the pictures into a fish pile and a shark pile.

3. Have students count the number of pictures in each pile. Extend the learning by having them add, subtract, multiply, or divide the two numbers.

4. Correct any misidentified pictures and ask students to explain why they mistook a fish for a shark or vice versa.

Name: _____   Date: _____

Fish and Sharks

DIRECTIONS: Sort your pictures into two piles, one for fish and one for sharks. Count the number of fish pictures and write the number in the fish circle. Count the number of shark pictures and write the number in the shark circle. Use both numbers to complete each math problem.

_____ fish pictures + _____ shark pictures = _____

_____ fish pictures x _____ shark pictures = _____

_____ fish pictures - _____ shark pictures = _____

_____ fish pictures ÷ _____ shark pictures = _____

Fish Dodgeball

MATERIALS

- Rubber balls
- Hula hoops
- Bowling pins

TEACHER INSTRUCTIONS

1. Place hula hoops around the gym (or play area). Inside each hoop, place one bowling pin upright. (The hula hoops represent fish nests, and the bowling pins represent fish.)

2. Place rubber balls around the gym (or play area).

3. Have a student stand by each hula hoop/nest to guard it, then ask the remaining students/players to form a line.

4. Give a signal for play to begin. The first student/player in line will retrieve a rubber ball and throw it at one of the bowling pins. The student/player guarding that "fish" will try to prevent the ball from knocking down the pin. The goal is to protect the fish.

5. When a fish (bowling pin) is knocked over, the player guarding that nest will place the pin upright and go to the back of the line. The player who knocked the pin over will take their place and be the new guard.

 For students with limited mobility or related health issues, consider modifying the game to best accommodate their needs.

Music Research Activity

MATERIALS

- Device with internet access
- "Music Research" notes page

TEACHER INSTRUCTIONS

1. Have students research different types of musical genres, including music from different countries or cultures.

2. Instruct students to create a slideshow or video presentation that highlights their research findings and includes audio samples of the music. Ask for volunteers to share their slideshows and videos with the class.

Name: _____   Date: _____

Music Research Notes

_____
_____
_____
_____
_____
_____
_____
_____
_____
_____
_____
_____
_____
_____
_____

Science Activity

MATERIALS

- "Mandarin Fish Research Notes" worksheet
- Pencils

TEACHER INSTRUCTIONS

1. Distribute the "Mandarin Fish Research Notes" worksheet.

2. Instruct students to use classroom and online research tools to gather facts and information about the Mandarin fish. Ask them to write a short essay summarizing their research findings. Encourage students to follow the outline provided on their worksheets when writing their essays.

3. Ask for volunteers to read their essays aloud.

Name: _____ Date: _____

Mandarin Fish Research Notes Worksheet

DIRECTIONS: Use classroom resources and websites to learn facts and information about the Mandarin fish. Write down your findings in the appropriate boxes, then use that information to write a five-paragraph essay about this colorful creature.

Paragraph 1: Introduction

Paragraph 2: Appearance

Paragraph 3: Habitat and Diet

Paragraph 4: Interesting Facts

Paragraph 5: Conclusion

Physical Appearance of the Mandarin Fish

MATERIALS

- "Physical Appearance of the Mandarin Fish" worksheet
- Computer/Laptop
- Internet access

TEACHER INSTRUCTIONS

1. Pass out the "Physical Appearance of the Mandarin Fish" worksheet.

2. Ask students to research the physical appearance of the Mandarin fish and answer the following questions:

    1. Do Mandarin fish have scales?
    2. What covers the body of the Mandarin fish?
    3. How do the vibrant colors of the Mandarin fish help them?
    4. How do the females and males differ in appearance?
    5. What is the average length of a Mandarin fish?
    6. What other additional facts or interesting information did you discover?

3. Have students create a slideshow or video presentation that highlights the answers to each question and any other information students learned. Ask for volunteers to share their slideshows and videos with the class.

 Do this activity in small groups of two, three, or four students.

Teacher + Counselor Activity Guide

Name: _____   Date: _____

Physical Appearance of the Mandarin Fish

DIRECTIONS: Research the physical appearance of the Mandarin fish and then answer the questions below. Use the answers and any other information you learn to create a slideshow or video presentation.

1. Do Mandarin fish have scales? _____
   _____
   _____

2. What covers the body of the Mandarin fish? _____
   _____
   _____

3. How do the vibrant colors of the Mandarin fish help them? _____
   _____
   _____
   _____

4. How do the females and males differ in appearance? _____
   _____
   _____

5. What is the average length of a Mandarin fish? _____
   _____

6. What other additional facts or interesting information did you discover? _____
   _____
   _____
   _____
   _____

Writing Activities

MATERIALS

- "Vocabulary Words" worksheet
- "Describe the Picture" worksheet
- "Finish the Sentence" worksheet
- "Would You Like to Be Friends with Someone Who Is Mean to Others?" worksheet
- "When You Did Not Feel Accepted by Others" worksheet
- Pencils

TEACHER INSTRUCTIONS

1. Pass out all five worksheets for students to complete at one time, or have them complete one worksheet per day during the school week.

2. Instruct students to fill out their worksheets and be prepared to discuss their answers as a group.

3. Allow enough time for students to complete the writing activity, then review and discuss the assignment as a group.

Name: _____ Date: _____

Vocabulary Words

DIRECTIONS: Write original sentences that include the vocabulary words listed below. Each word needs to be used at least once, and a sentence can have more than one vocabulary word in it. When all the words have been used in sentences, draw a comic strip or a picture that represents or reflects as many of the vocabulary words as possible.

Vocabulary Words: Report, Teacher, Bully, Mean, Feel, Kindness, Friend, Care, Different, Acceptance

_____
_____
_____
_____
_____
_____
_____
_____
_____
_____
_____
_____
_____
_____
_____

Name: _____   Date: _____

Describe the Picture

DIRECTIONS: Look at the picture and then fill in the worksheet.

1. This is a picture of what? _____
   _____

2. What is happening in the picture? _____
   _____
   _____

3. Where do you think this picture was taken (setting/location)? _____
   _____
   _____

4. Write an original sentence that includes your answers to the questions above: _____
   _____
   _____
   _____
   _____
   _____
   _____
   _____
   _____
   _____
   _____

Name: _____ Date: _____

Finish the Sentence

DIRECTIONS: Complete the sentence and then draw a picture to match your sentence.

I AM UNIQUE BECAUSE _____
_____
_____
_____
_____
_____

Name: _____ Date: _____

Would You Like to Be Friends with Someone Who Is Mean to Others?

DIRECTIONS: Fill in the worksheet by answering yes or no if you would like to be friends with someone who is mean to others. Write down three reasons to support your answer.

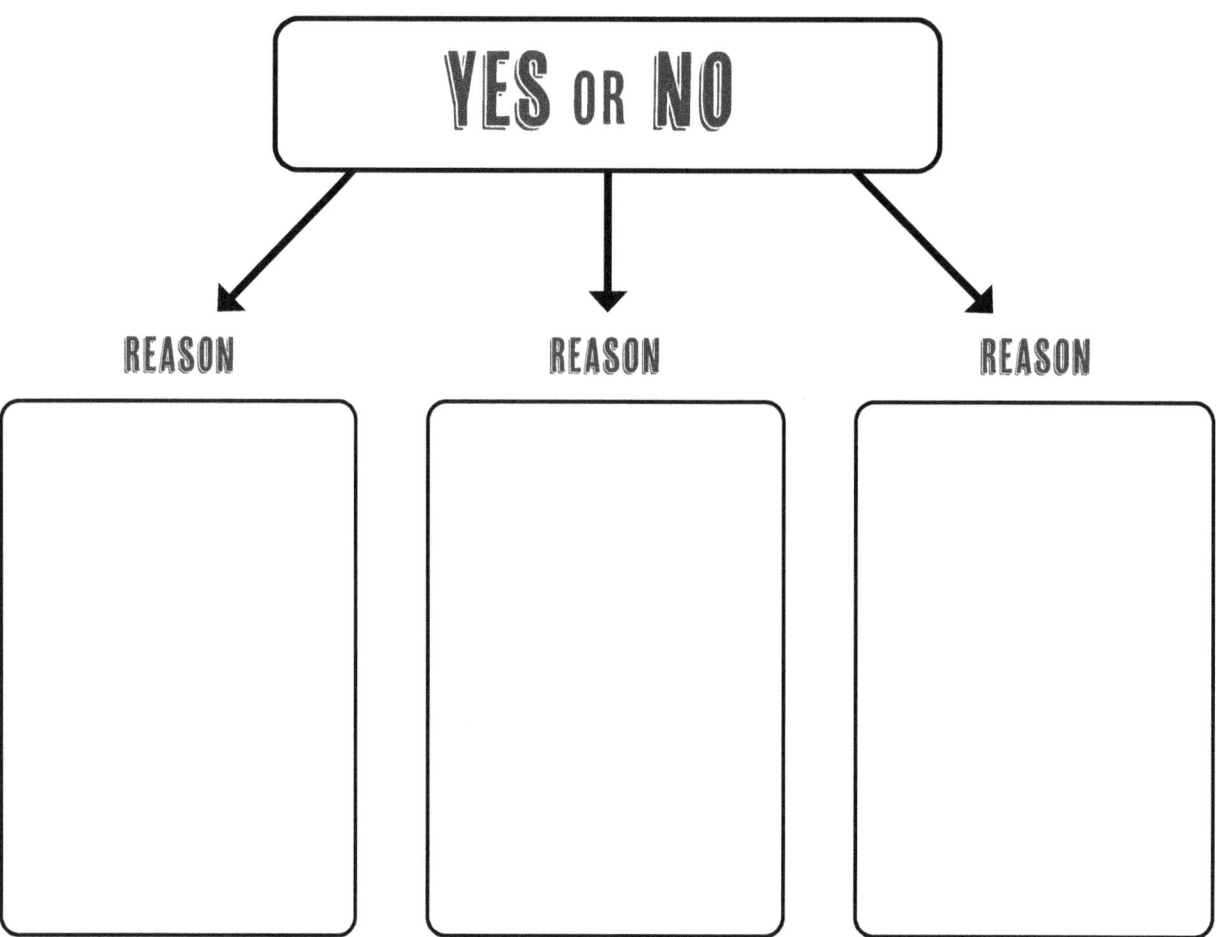

Name: _____ Date: _____

When You Did Not Feel Accepted by Others

DIRECTIONS: Read the text and then answer the questions.

TEXT: Think about a situation where you felt like you did not fit in or were not accepted by others.

1. What was the situation? _____
_____

2. How did you feel in that moment? _____
_____
_____

3. What do you wish had happened instead? _____
_____
_____

4. What would the situation have looked like or felt like if you had been welcomed and accepted? _____
_____
_____
_____
_____

NOTES

EPAULETTE SHARK

SKILL
SHAKTI, AN EPAULETTE SHARK, IS BULLIED FOR NOT BEING A "BIG, POWERFUL SHARK." HOWEVER, SHE IS VERY CONFIDENT IN HER SKIN. SHE KNOWS SHE CANNOT CONTROL WHAT OTHERS SAY, JUST HOW SHE RESPONDS. SHE ALSO KNOWS THAT IT'S OKAY TO BE DIFFERENT. SHAKTI TEACHES US HOW TO STAND UP TO BULLYING AND UNDERSTAND WHAT WE CAN AND CANNOT CONTROL.

EPAULETTE SHARK
Assertiveness and Accountability

The name Shakti means power.

*Shakti Shark has the unique ability to walk,
which sometimes causes the other sea creatures to talk.*

*Shakti used to get made fun of for her unique skill,
but she learned not to let the bullies get a thrill.*

*Every day, the bullies had a mean remark,
"Haha, you're not a big and powerful shark."*

*One day, she told herself what they were saying was not okay.
Shakti Shark was not going to let them talk to her that way.*

*There are some things in life you cannot control,
such as another creature's words, actions, thoughts, or goals.*

*You cannot control the weather, or even the past,
but you can have a say if you are being harassed.*

*You have control over your word choices and reactions.
Also over your thoughts, attitudes, and actions.*

*While you cannot control what others say,
you should not let them cause you to feel gray.*

*If someone says something mean to you,
you need to tell them your point of view.*

Teacher + Counselor Activity Guide

Q: Can an epaulette shark walk?
A: Yes!

TRIVIA QUESTION

*"It hurts my feelings when you say I'm not a big, powerful shark.
Frodo Fish and Ollie Octopus, please stop making that remark."*

You could also try to crack some hilarious jokes.
Confidence can reduce the power of mean folks.

Ignoring is another very powerful tool.
Not reacting will usually decrease the mean fuel.

If someone continues to be mean,
you need to tell an adult about the scene.

It is important to have an adult step in,
because bullies should never be allowed to win.

You have control over your emotions,
so don't listen to their mean commotions.

At the end of each and every day,
you are the only one with a say.

You know who you really are.
You know inside you are a star.

Circle of Control Collage

MATERIALS

- Magazines and other printed materials
- "Circle of Control Collage" worksheet (or Drawing Paper/Poster Board)*
- Colored Pencils/Crayons/Markers
- Glue/Tape
- Scissors

TEACHER INSTRUCTIONS

1. Gather a variety of magazines and other printed materials, then distribute them to each student (or group).

2. Instruct students to look through the material to find words and images representing things they can control and things they cannot control. Have them cut out the words and images.

3. Review with students the directions on the worksheet. Students will glue or tape the cutouts of things they can control inside the circle. The cutouts of things they cannot control go outside the circle.

*If there is not enough space inside or outside the circle on the worksheet, provide drawing paper or poster board as an alternative.

Teacher + Counselor Activity Guide

Name: _____ Date: _____

Circle of Control Collage

DIRECTIONS: Inside the circle, glue or tape cutouts of the words and images that represent things you can control. Outside the circle, glue or tape the pictures and words that represent things you cannot control.

Shakti Epaulette Shark Discussion Questions

MATERIALS

- Pencils
- "Discussion Questions" worksheet

TEACHER INSTRUCTIONS

1. Pass out the "Discussion Questions" worksheet.
2. Instruct students to complete the worksheet by answering the questions.
3. Read the questions aloud and discuss possible answers as a group.

CLASS/GROUP DISCUSSION QUESTIONS

1. Is it ever okay to make fun of someone for being different?
2. What are examples of things you cannot control?
3. What are examples of things you can control?
4. How can you stand up for yourself when someone is being mean?
5. What should you do if someone continues to be mean to you every day?
6. Who are the trusted adults in your life whom you can talk to when you're having problems at school, with friends, or with others?

Name: _____ Date: _____

Discussion Questions

DIRECTIONS: In the space provided, answer the following questions. Be prepared to discuss your answers with the group.

1. Is it ever okay to make fun of someone for being different? _____
   _____
   _____
   _____

2. What are examples of things you cannot control? _____
   _____
   _____
   _____

3. What are examples of things you can control? _____
   _____
   _____
   _____

4. How can you stand up for yourself when someone is being mean? _____
   _____
   _____
   _____

5. What should you do if someone continues to be mean to you every day? _____
   _____
   _____
   _____

Discussion Questions continued

6. Who are the trusted adults in your life whom you can talk to when you're having problems at school, with friends, or with others? _____

_____

_____

_____

Teacher + Counselor Activity Guide

Circle of Control Drawing Activity

MATERIALS

- Colored Pencils/Crayons/Markers
- "Circle of Control" Paper/Poster Board

TEACHER INSTRUCTIONS

1. Distribute the "Circle of Control" paper/poster board.

2. Review with students the directions for the poster.

3. Ask for volunteers to show and explain their drawings.

Under the Sea Lessons for Life – Volume 2

Name: _____ Date: _____

Circle of Control Poster

DIRECTIONS: Draw a circle of control. Inside the circle, draw or write things you can control. Outside the circle, draw or write things you cannot control.

Math Activity

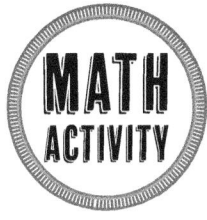

MATERIALS

- Pencil
- "Epaulette Shark Math" worksheet

TEACHER INSTRUCTIONS

1. Pass out the "Epaulette Shark Math" worksheet.

2. Instruct students to answer the word problem, then review the answer as a class. Extend the learning by including your own math or word problems on the worksheet.

Name: _____ Date: _____

Epaulette Shark Math

DIRECTIONS: Solve the following word problem and show your work.

1. The epaulette shark can survive extended periods of time without oxygen. If this shark can go 1.5 hours without oxygen, how many times must it breathe in a 24-hour period?

2. Bonus Problem:

3. Bonus Problem:

Name: _____ **ANSWER KEY** _____ Date: _____

Epaulette Shark Math

DIRECTIONS: Solve the following word problem and show your work.

1. The epaulette shark can survive extended periods of time without oxygen. If this shark can go 1.5 hours without oxygen, how many times must it breathe in a 24-hour period?

    24 ÷ 1.5 = 16

2. Bonus Problem:

3. Bonus Problem:

Fish, Fish... Shark!

MATERIALS

- Gym/Play Area

TEACHER INSTRUCTIONS

1. Ask students to sit in a circle. (They will be playing a renamed version of the game, "Duck, Duck, Goose.")

2. Choose one student to be Player 1, or "It."

3. Instruct Player 1 to walk around the circle of students, gently tapping the top of their heads (or shoulders) while saying, "Fish, Fish, Fish...." When Player 1 says, "Shark," the student who was tapped is now the Shark and must stand up and chase Player 1 around the circle. If the Shark can tag Player 1 before Player 1 sits down in the Shark's spot, Player 1 remains "It" and the game continues. If Player 1 reaches the Shark's spot without being tagged, the Shark becomes "It." Continue playing until everyone has had a chance to be the Shark.

 For students with limited mobility or related health issues, consider modifying the game to best accommodate their needs.

Teacher + Counselor Activity Guide

Picture the Lyrics Musical Drawing

MATERIALS

- Music Player
- Colored Pencils/Crayons/Markers
- "Picture the Lyrics" Drawing Paper/Poster Board

TEACHER INSTRUCTIONS

1. Choose a song (with age-appropriate lyrics) and play it for everyone to hear. For deaf or hard-of-hearing youth, provide a print out of the lyrics.

2. Ask students to listen carefully to (or read) the song lyrics and then draw a picture inspired by the words in the song.

3. Ask for volunteers to share their drawings with the group.

Name: _____   Date: _____

Picture the Lyrics

DIRECTIONS: Draw a picture based on the words (or lyrics) in a song. Be prepared to share your drawing with the group.

Teacher + Counselor Activity Guide

Science Activity

MATERIALS

- "Epaulette Shark Research Notes" worksheet
- Pencils

TEACHER INSTRUCTIONS

1. Distribute the "Epaulette Shark Research Notes" worksheet.

2. Instruct students to use classroom and online research tools to gather facts and information about the epaulette shark. Ask them to write a short essay summarizing their research findings. Encourage students to follow the outline provided on their worksheets when writing their essays.

3. Ask for volunteers to read their essays aloud.

Name: _____ Date: _____

Epaulette Shark Research Notes

DIRECTIONS: Use classroom resources and websites to learn facts and information about the epaulette shark. Write down your findings in the appropriate boxes, then use that information to write a five-paragraph essay about this fascinating creature.

Paragraph 1: Introduction

Paragraph 2: Appearance

Paragraph 3: Habitat and Diet

Paragraph 4: Interesting Facts

Paragraph 5: Conclusion

Teacher + Counselor Activity Guide

The Walking Shark

MATERIALS

- "The Walking Shark" worksheet
- Computer/Laptop
- Internet access

TEACHER INSTRUCTIONS

1. Pass out the "The Walking Shark" worksheet.

2. Ask students to research the epaulette shark and answer the following questions:

    1. How do epaulette sharks walk?
    2. What can an epaulette shark do to conserve energy?
    3. Where do epaulette sharks typically walk?
    4. Do epaulette sharks also swim?
    5. How long can an epaulette shark go without oxygen?
    6. What other additional facts or interesting information did you discover?

3. Have students create a slideshow or video presentation that highlights the answers to each question and any other information students learned. Ask for volunteers to share their slideshows and videos with the class.

Name: _____ Date: _____

The Walking Shark

DIRECTIONS: Research how epaulette sharks walk and then answer the questions below. Use the answers and any other information you learn to create a slideshow or video presentation.

1. How do epaulette sharks walk? _____
_____
_____

2. What can an epaulette shark do to conserve energy? _____
_____
_____

3. Where do epaulette sharks typically walk? _____
_____
_____

4. Do epaulette sharks also swim? _____
_____
_____

5. How long can an epaulette shark go without oxygen? _____
_____
_____

6. What other additional facts or interesting information did you discover? _____
_____
_____
_____
_____

Writing Activities

MATERIALS

- "Vocabulary Words" worksheet
- "Describe the Picture" worksheet
- "Finish the Sentence" worksheet
- "Would You Stand Up to a Bully?" worksheet
- "When Someone Was Mean" worksheet
- Pencils

TEACHER INSTRUCTIONS

1. Pass out all five worksheets for students to complete at one time, or have them complete one worksheet per day during the school week.

2. Instruct students to fill out their worksheets and be prepared to discuss their answers as a group.

3. Allow enough time for students to complete the writing activity, then review and discuss the assignment as a group.

Name: _____ Date: _____

Vocabulary Words

DIRECTIONS: Write original sentences that include the vocabulary words listed below. Each word needs to be used at least once, and a sentence can have more than one vocabulary word in it. When all the words have been used in sentences, draw a comic strip or a picture that represents or reflects as many of the vocabulary words as possible.

Vocabulary Words: Can, Cannot, Control, Words, Actions, Thoughts, Reactions, Attitude, Other, People

_____
_____
_____
_____
_____
_____
_____
_____
_____
_____
_____
_____
_____
_____

Teacher + Counselor Activity Guide

Name: _____   Date: _____

Describe the Picture

DIRECTIONS: Look at the picture and then fill in the worksheet.

1. This is a picture of what? _____
   _____

2. What is happening in the picture? _____
   _____
   _____

3. Where do you think this picture was taken (setting/location)? _____
   _____
   _____

4. Write an original sentence that includes your answers to the questions above:
   _____
   _____
   _____
   _____
   _____
   _____
   _____
   _____
   _____
   _____
   _____
   _____

Name: _____ Date: _____

Finish the Sentence

DIRECTIONS: Complete the sentence and then draw a picture to match your sentence.

I CAN CONTROL MY _____
_____
_____
_____
_____
_____

Teacher + Counselor Activity Guide

Name: _____ Date: _____

Would You Stand Up to a Bully?

DIRECTIONS: Fill in the worksheet by answering yes or no if you would stand up to a bully. Write down three reasons to support your answer.

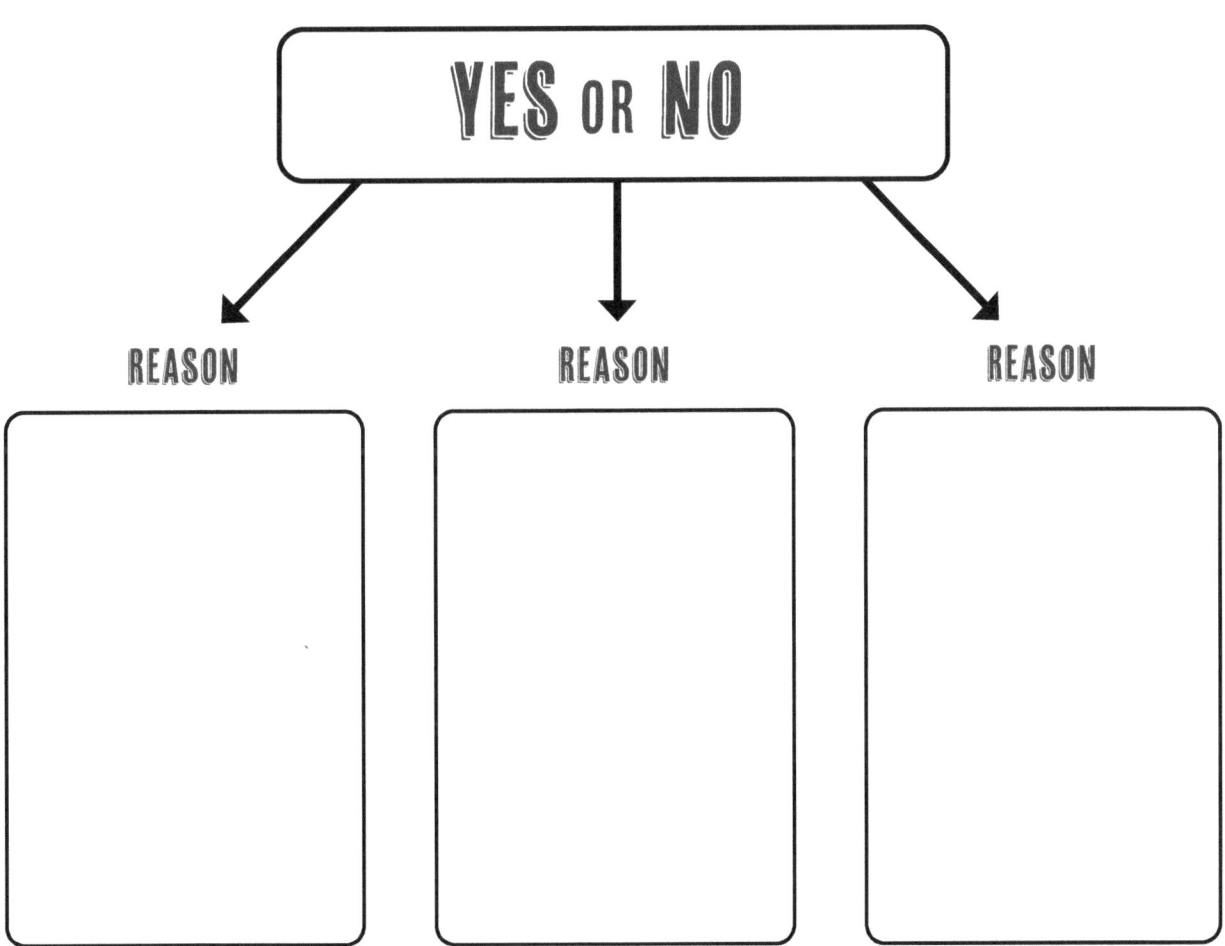

Name: _____ Date: _____

When Someone Was Mean

DIRECTIONS: Read the text and then answer the questions.

TEXT: Think about a situation where someone was mean to you.

1. What did the person say or do? _____
   _____

2. How did you feel in that moment? _____
   _____
   _____

3. How did you react? _____
   _____
   _____

4. If that same situation happens again, how will you respond? _____
   _____
   _____
   _____
   _____
   _____
   _____

NUDIBRANCH

SKILL

NIKO, A NUDIBRANCH, IS AN EXCELLENT PROBLEM SOLVER. NIKO AND SEABORN BRITTLE STAR MAKE AN EXCELLENT TEAM. FRODO MANDARIN FISH WANTS NIKO TO JOIN IN THE BULLYING, BUT NIKO RESISTS THE PEER PRESSURE. HE STANDS UP TO FRODO AND GETS HELP FROM A GROWN-UP. NIKO NUDIBRANCH TEACHES US THE DIFFERENCE BETWEEN TATTLING AND REPORTING.

NUDIBRANCH
Problem Solving and Bullying

The name Niko means person of victory.

*Niko Nudibranch is known for his versatility.
Changing shapes and colors is his unique ability.*

*This special skill makes him stand out.
All the others are jealous, no doubt.*

*Frodo Mandarin Fish and Ollie Octopus wanted Niko to join their team,
but being a member was not part of Niko Nudibranch's dream.*

*Frodo and Ollie were never-ever kind,
so Niko respectfully declined.*

*Frodo and Ollie would not stop.
They threatened Niko and wanted to make him pop.*

*Frodo and Ollie wanted Niko to help them be mean,
so Niko searched for an adult who could intervene.*

*Niko ignored them and swam away,
because what Frodo and Ollie were doing was not okay.*

*He headed toward his caring teachers,
while the duo screamed, "You're a tattling creature!"*

*Niko knew what Frodo and Ollie said was not true,
and he decided to let his teachers deal with those two.*

*There's a difference between a tattle and a report.
Only a report needs a kind, loving grown-up's support.*

*A tattle is when you want to get a creature in trouble.
Like when someone takes two juices so you blurt, "He took double."*

*A tattle you can usually fix by yourself.
For example, "Please do not touch my stuff on the shelf."*

*If someone accidentally bumps you in line,
you can handle that problem on your own just fine.*

*If no sea creatures are being hurt,
you do not need to send an alert.*

*However, reporting is crucial when someone is in danger.
Like if you are being hurt or you were approached by a stranger.*

*If you see someone hurt,
you are allowed to blurt.*

*If you tell someone to stop but they still continue,
you need to use bravery and the strength within you.*

*It is important to tell a grown-up what occurred,
so that they can put an end to the bullying, undeterred.*

*Bullying and violence are never okay.
Always report it, no matter what others say.*

Q: Nudibranchs also are known as: sea slimers/sea shells/sea slugs/sea snakes

A: Sea Slugs

TRIVIA QUESTION

Clay Nudibranch

MATERIALS

- Clay blocks or balls
- Variety of clay tools (rolling pin, plastic knife, cookie cutters, sponge, etc.)
- Paint/Paint Brushes

TEACHER INSTRUCTIONS

1. Show an image of a nudibranch.

2. Distribute clay blocks or balls to students, then instruct them to create a replica of a nudibranch.

3. Have students paint their replicas in unique colors, once the clay is dry.

Teacher + Counselor Activity Guide

Niko Nudibranch Discussion Questions

MATERIALS

- Pencils
- "Discussion Questions" worksheet

TEACHER INSTRUCTIONS

1. Pass out the "Discussion Questions" worksheet.
2. Instruct students to fill out the worksheet by answering the questions.
3. Read the questions aloud and discuss possible answers as a group.

CLASS/GROUP DISCUSSION QUESTIONS

1. What special skills do you have?
2. What should you do if someone asks you to do something mean, hurtful, or that makes you feel uncomfortable?
3. What does it mean to report someone's behavior or report a situation?
4. What is tattling?
5. How can you solve a problem by yourself?
6. Who can you talk to at school if you need to report something?

Under the Sea Lessons for Life – Volume 2

Name: _____   Date: _____

Discussion Questions

DIRECTIONS: In the space provided, answer the following questions. Be prepared to discuss your answers with the group.

1. What special skills do you have? _____
   _____
   _____

2. What should you do if someone asks you to do something mean, hurtful, or that makes you feel uncomfortable? _____
   _____

3. What does it mean to report someone's behavior or report a situation? _____
   _____
   _____

4. What is tattling? _____
   _____

5. How can you solve a problem by yourself? _____
   _____
   _____

6. Who can you talk to at school if you need to report something? _____
   _____
   _____

Drawing Activity

MATERIALS

- Colored Pencils/Crayons/Markers
- "Reporting vs. Tattling" Paper/Poster Board

TEACHER INSTRUCTIONS

1. Distribute the "Reporting vs. Tattling" paper/poster board.

2. Review with students the directions for the poster.

3. Ask for volunteers to show and explain their drawings.

Name: _____ Date: _____

Reporting vs. Tattling Poster

DIRECTIONS: Draw and describe the difference between reporting and tattling.

Math Activity

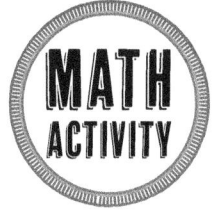

MATERIALS

- Computer/Laptop
- Internet access
- "Shapes and Patterns" worksheet
- Pencils

TEACHER INSTRUCTIONS

1. Display an image of a nudibranch (or display different, multiple images of nudibranchs; one for each student).

2. Instruct students to take a close look at the image and then answer the questions on their worksheet.

3. Hand out the "Shapes and Patterns" worksheet.

4. Allow at least 20 to 30 minutes for students to complete the activity.

 Add an additional math problem or question to the worksheet that is tailored to your students' skill level.

Name: _____ Date: _____

Shapes and Patterns

DIRECTIONS: Look closely at the image of the nudibranch, then answer or solve each question. Be prepared to explain your answers.

1. How many different colors do you see on the nudibranch? _____
   _____

2. Name the colors: _____
   _____

3. How many different patterns do you see on the nudibranch? _____
   _____

4. Name the shapes of the patterns (ovals, stripes, rectangles, etc.): _____
   _____

5. Nudibranchs can regenerate (or regrow) parts of their body, such as their finger-like tentacles. If the nudibranch shown in the picture loses half its tentacles, how many tentacles remain? _____
   _____

5. *Bonus equation/question:* _____
   _____

Sea Creature Yoga

MATERIALS

- Gym/Play Area
- Yoga Mats

TEACHER INSTRUCTIONS

1. Lead an exercise class that incorporates stretching, breathing, and yoga poses.

2. Use characters from the story – Frodo Fish, Shakti Shark, Niko Nudibranch, Seabourn Star, and Casey Clam – to name the various stretches, poses, or breathing exercises you want students to perform. For example, you might say, "Pretend to be a shark." Then explain or demonstrate the following pose:

    - Lay face down on your belly.
    - Clasp your hands behind your back, like a fin.
    - Focus your eyes straight ahead, then lift your chest and legs.
    - Hold the pose for three to five seconds, then slowly bring your chest, arms, and legs back down.

3. For a breathing exercise, you might say, "Do Niko Nudibranch nostril breathing." Then explain or demonstrate the following technique:

    - Close your eyes.
    - Use your fingers to close one nostril.
    - Breathe in through the open nostril.
    - Move your fingers and close the other nostril.
    - Breathe out through the open nostril.
    - Continue to alternate inhaling and exhaling through one nostril.

4. For a stretching exercise, you might say, "Let's do a flat Seabourn Star pose." Then explain or demonstrate the following stretch:

- Lay on your back with your legs straight and slightly apart.
- Stretch your arms outward, with your palms facing upward.
- Close your eyes and take a deep breath in.
- Hold your breath for five seconds.
- Slowly exhale.

 For students with limited mobility or related health issues, consider modifying the exercises to best accommodate their needs.

Teacher + Counselor Activity Guide

Musical Chairs: Tattling vs. Reporting

MATERIALS

- Gym/Play Area
- Chairs
- Music Player

TEACHER INSTRUCTIONS

1. Arrange chairs in a circle, with one fewer chair than the number of players.

2. Explain the directions: When the music begins, calmly walk around the circle of chairs. When the music stops, sit down on an empty chair as quickly as possible. The player left standing will be asked to decide if a situation is tattling or reporting. After answering, the player will leave the game and remove a chair. The game continues until only one player remains.

3. Use the "Is It Tattling or Reporting?" scenarios during the game or create your own:

Is it TATTLING or REPORTING?	*You see someone cut in front of the line, so you tell the teacher.*
Is it TATTLING or REPORTING?	*Someone yells, "There's a fire in the trash can!"*
Is it TATTLING or REPORTING?	*You tell the teacher someone hit you.*
Is it TATTLING or REPORTING?	*You tell the teacher someone is bleeding.*
Is it TATTLING or REPORTING?	*A classmate falls and gets hurt, and you tell an adult.*
Is it TATTLING or REPORTING?	*You tell the teacher someone took the crayon you wanted.*
Is it TATTLING or REPORTING?	*You tell the teacher your friend wants to read at recess instead of playing with you.*
Is it TATTLING or REPORTING?	*You tell an adult that Benny is throwing rocks at people.*
Is it TATTLING or REPORTING?	*You tell the teacher the person sitting across from you is drawing pictures in their notebook.*
Is it TATTLING or REPORTING?	*You tell the teacher Essie walked down the wrong side of the stairwell.*
Is it TATTLING or REPORTING?	*You tell the teacher that DeeDee called CeeCee really mean names at recess.*
Is it TATTLING or REPORTING?	*You tell the teacher Finn is using the wrong color crayon.*
Is it TATTLING or REPORTING?	*Bakari accidentally bumps into you, and you tell the teacher.*

Science Activity

MATERIALS

- "Nudibranch Research Notes" worksheet
- Pencils

TEACHER INSTRUCTIONS

1. Distribute the "Nudibranch Research Notes" worksheet.

2. Instruct students to use classroom and online research tools to gather facts and information about the nudibranch. Ask them to write a short essay summarizing their research findings. Encourage students to follow the outline provided on their worksheets when writing their essays.

3. Ask for volunteers to read their essays aloud.

Teacher + Counselor Activity Guide

Name: _____ Date: _____

Nudibranch Research Notes

DIRECTIONS: Use classroom resources and websites to learn facts and information about the nudibranch. Write down your findings in the appropriate boxes, then use that information to write a five-paragraph essay about this soft-bodied creature.

1 **Paragraph 1:** Introduction

2 **Paragraph 2:** Appearance

3 **Paragraph 3:** Habitat and Diet

4 **Paragraph 4:** Interesting Facts

5 **Paragraph 5:** Conclusion

Fun Facts about Nudibranchs

MATERIALS

- "Fun Facts about Nudibranchs" worksheet
- Computer/Laptop
- Internet access

TEACHER INSTRUCTIONS

1. Pass out the "Fun Facts about Nudibranchs" worksheet.

2. Ask students to research the nudibranch and answer the following questions:

    1. What type of animal is the nudibranch?
    2. What makes the nudibranch unique?
    3. How long do nudibranchs live?
    4. How do nudibranchs communicate with each other?
    5. What is unique about the appearance of their eggs?
    6. What other additional facts or interesting information did you discover?

3. Have students create a slideshow or video presentation that highlights the answers to each question and any other information students learned. Ask for volunteers to share their slideshows and videos with the class.

Name: _____   Date: _____

Fun Facts about Nudibranchs

DIRECTIONS: Research interesting facts about the nudibranch and then answer the questions below. Use the answers and any other information you learn to create a slideshow or video presentation.

1. What type of animal is the nudibranch? _____
   _____
   _____

2. What makes the nudibranch unique? _____
   _____
   _____

3. How long do nudibranchs live? _____
   _____
   _____

4. How do nudibranchs communicate with each other? _____
   _____
   _____

5. What is unique about the appearance of their eggs? _____
   _____
   _____
   _____

6. What other additional facts or interesting information did you discover? _____
   _____
   _____
   _____

Writing Activities

MATERIALS

- "Vocabulary Words" worksheet
- "Describe the Picture" worksheet
- "Finish the Sentence" worksheet
- "Do You Think Bullying Should Be Reported?" worksheet
- "Tattling and Reporting" worksheet
- Pencils

TEACHER INSTRUCTIONS

1. Pass out all five worksheets for students to complete at one time, or have them complete one worksheet per day during the school week.

2. Instruct students to fill out their worksheets and be prepared to discuss their answers as a group.

3. Allow enough time for students to complete the writing activity, then review and discuss the assignment as a group.

Name: _____ Date: _____

Vocabulary Words

DIRECTIONS: Write original sentences that include the vocabulary words listed below. Each word needs to be used at least once, and a sentence can have more than one vocabulary word in it. When all the words have been used in sentences, draw a comic strip or a picture that represents or reflects as many of the vocabulary words as possible.

Vocabulary Words: Tattle, Report, Adult, Trouble, Problem, Accident, Danger, Hurt, Alert, Brave

_____
_____
_____
_____
_____
_____
_____
_____
_____
_____
_____
_____
_____
_____

Under the Sea Lessons for Life – Volume 2

Name: _____ Date: _____

Describe the Picture

DIRECTIONS: Look at the picture and then fill in the worksheet.

1. This is a picture of what? _____
   _____

2. What is happening in the picture? _____
   _____
   _____

3. Where do you think this picture was taken (setting/location)? _____
   _____
   _____

4. Write an original sentence that includes your answers to the questions above: _____
   _____
   _____
   _____
   _____
   _____
   _____
   _____
   _____
   _____
   _____

72

Name: _____ Date: _____

Finish the Sentence

DIRECTIONS: Complete the sentence and then draw a picture to match your sentence.

I WILL TELL, OR REPORT TO, A TRUSTED ADULT IF _____
_____
_____
_____
_____
_____

Name: _____ Date: _____

Do You Think Bullying Should Be Reported?

DIRECTIONS: Fill in the worksheet by answering yes or no if you think bullying should be reported. Write down three reasons to support your answer.

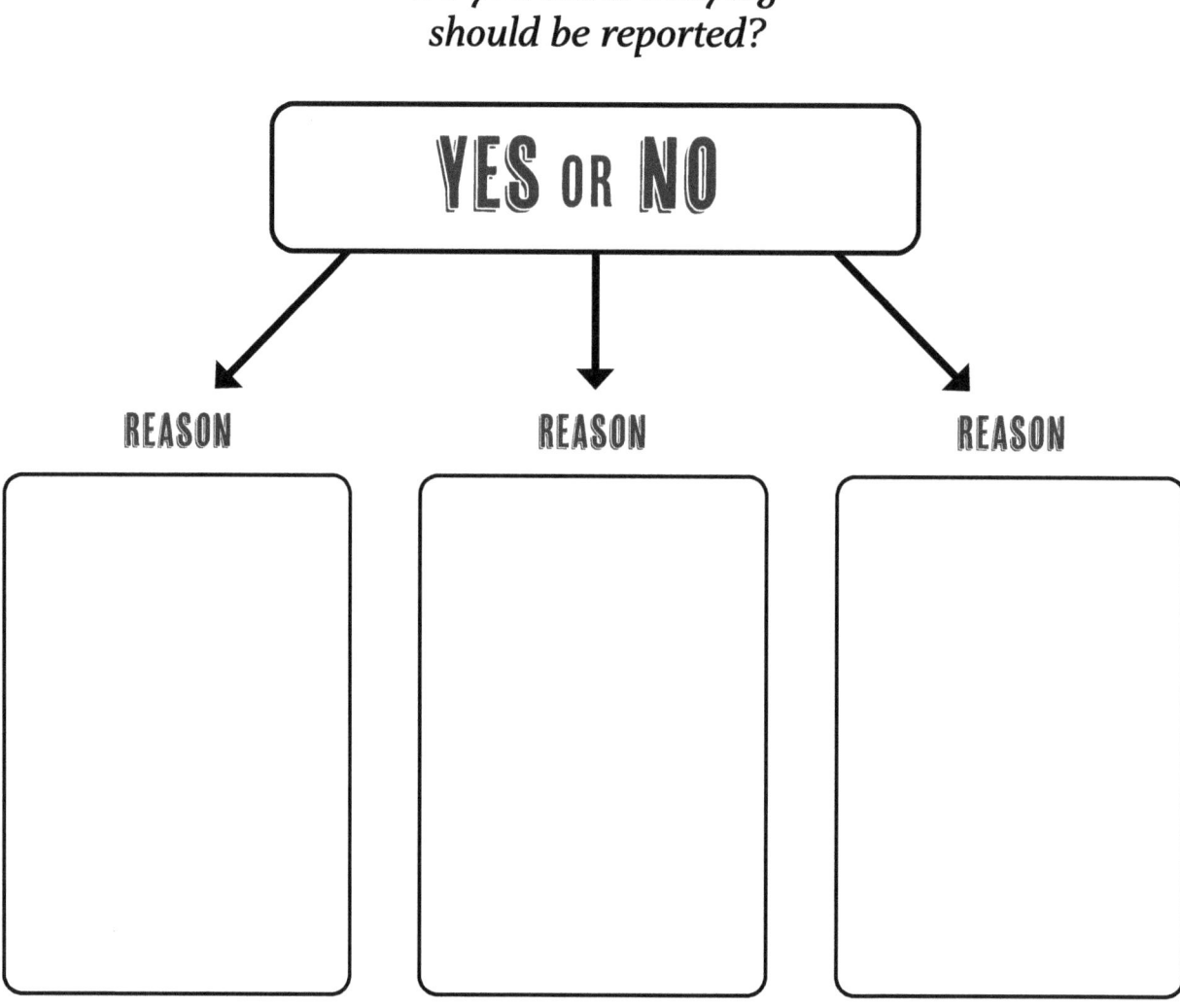

Name: _____ Date: _____

Tattling and Reporting

DIRECTIONS: Read the text and then answer the questions.

TEXT: Think about a situation when you or someone tattled. Then think about a situation when you or someone reported.

1. What was the tattling situation? Did you tattle or were you tattled on? _____
   _____

2. What happened after you (or someone) tattled or were tattled on? _____
   _____
   _____

3. What was the reporting situation? Did you report, or did someone report you? _____
   _____
   _____

4. What happened after you (or someone) reported or were reported on? _____
   _____
   _____
   _____
   _____

NOTES

BRITTLE STAR

SKILL — SEABORN, A BRITTLE STAR, IS AN UNDERSEA SUPERHERO. HE IS AN EXCELLENT PROBLEM SOLVER AND TEAM PLAYER. SEABORN TEACHES US THE IMPORTANCE OF TEAMWORK.

BRITTLE STAR
Compromising and Teamwork

The name Seaborn means sea warrior.

Seaborn Star is the superhero of the sea.
All the other sea creatures strongly agree.

He is as flexible as a slithering snake,
and he can still function if his arms should happen to break.

His best friend, Niko, helps him when trouble strikes.
The two of them have many similar likes.

But it wasn't all rainbows in the beginning.
The only thing Seaborn cared about was winning.

Seaborn Star wanted to win all on his own,
but he soon learned it was boring being alone.

He needed a partner to help him succeed.
Niko would be the perfect teammate, indeed.

Seaborn Star learned working together means he cannot always have his way.
He also needs to consider what his best friend, Niko, has to say.

Teamwork is all about appreciating individual strengths,
combining your unique talents so you can reach greater lengths.

There is no "I" in team,
when teamwork is your dream.

Q: How many jaws are in the mouth of a brittle star?

A: 5

Teamwork requires a lot of sharing,
and you also need to be caring.

You need to listen to each other's suggestions,
and answer any and all of each other's questions.

You need to bounce ideas around
until the best solution is found.

You may not always agree with your best friend,
but you need to stick together till the end.

Compromise is key,
if we truly are a "we."

Teamwork truly is the best;
you should put it to the test.

Brittle Star Mosaic

MATERIALS

- Paper/Poster Board
- "Brittle Star Mosaic" Poster
- Colored Construction Paper (or white paper)
- Colored Pencils/Crayons/Markers
- Scissors
- Glue

TEACHER INSTRUCTIONS

1. Group students into teams of two or three.

2. Hand out sheets of construction paper of various colors (yellow, blue, green, etc.) to each team. Or, hand out sheets of white paper and ask the teams to color each sheet a different color. Some sheets also can be multicolored.

3. Instruct each team to tear up their colored sheets into various sizes and then put them together to create a mosaic of a brittle star on the ocean floor.

4. Lead a group discussion after all teams have created their mosaics. Ask for volunteers to answer the following questions:
    - How well did your team work together?
    - Did your teammate(s) show kindness and respect?
    - How did you support each other during the project?

Teacher + Counselor Activity Guide

Name: _____   Date: _____

Brittle Star Mosaic Poster

DIRECTIONS: Tear up colored sheets of paper and then glue them on the poster to create a mosaic of a brittle star resting on the ocean floor.

81

Seaborn Brittle Star Discussion Questions

MATERIALS

- Pencils
- "Discussion Questions" worksheet

TEACHER INSTRUCTIONS

1. Pass out the "Discussion Questions" worksheet.

2. Instruct students to fill out the worksheet by answering the questions.

3. Read the questions aloud and discuss possible answers as a group.

CLASS/GROUP DISCUSSION QUESTIONS

1. If you are playing on a team or working in a group, can you always have things your way? Explain why or why not.

2. What does it mean to compromise?

3. What makes someone a good teammate?

4. Why is it important to appreciate individual strengths?

5. Why is it important to listen to teammates' or team members' thoughts, opinions, and suggestions?

6. Is it okay to disagree with your teammates or team members sometimes? Explain why or why not.

7. Is it ever okay to be mean or disruptive when you have a disagreement?

Name: _____ Date: _____

Discussion Questions

DIRECTIONS: In the space provided, answer the following questions. Be prepared to discuss your answers with the group.

1. If you are playing on a team or working in a group, can you always have things your way? Explain why or why not. _____
   _____
   _____

2. What does it mean to compromise? _____
   _____
   _____

3. What makes someone a good teammate? _____
   _____
   _____
   _____

4. Why is it important to appreciate individual strengths? _____
   _____
   _____
   _____

5. Why is it important to listen to teammates' or team members' thoughts, opinions, and suggestions? _____
   _____
   _____
   _____

Discussion Questions continued

6. Is it okay to disagree with your teammates or team members sometimes? Explain why or why not. _____

_____

_____

_____

7. Is it ever okay to be mean or disruptive when you have a disagreement? _____

_____

_____

_____

Drawing Activity

MATERIALS

- Colored Pencils/Crayons/Markers
- "A Good Teammate" Paper/Poster Board

TEACHER INSTRUCTIONS

1. Distribute the "A Good Teammate" paper/poster board.

2. Review with students the directions for the poster.

3. Ask for volunteers to show and explain their drawings.

Name: _____ Date: _____

A Good Teammate Poster

DIRECTIONS: Draw a picture of what you think a good teammate looks like and include words or phrases that describe what it means to be a good teammate.

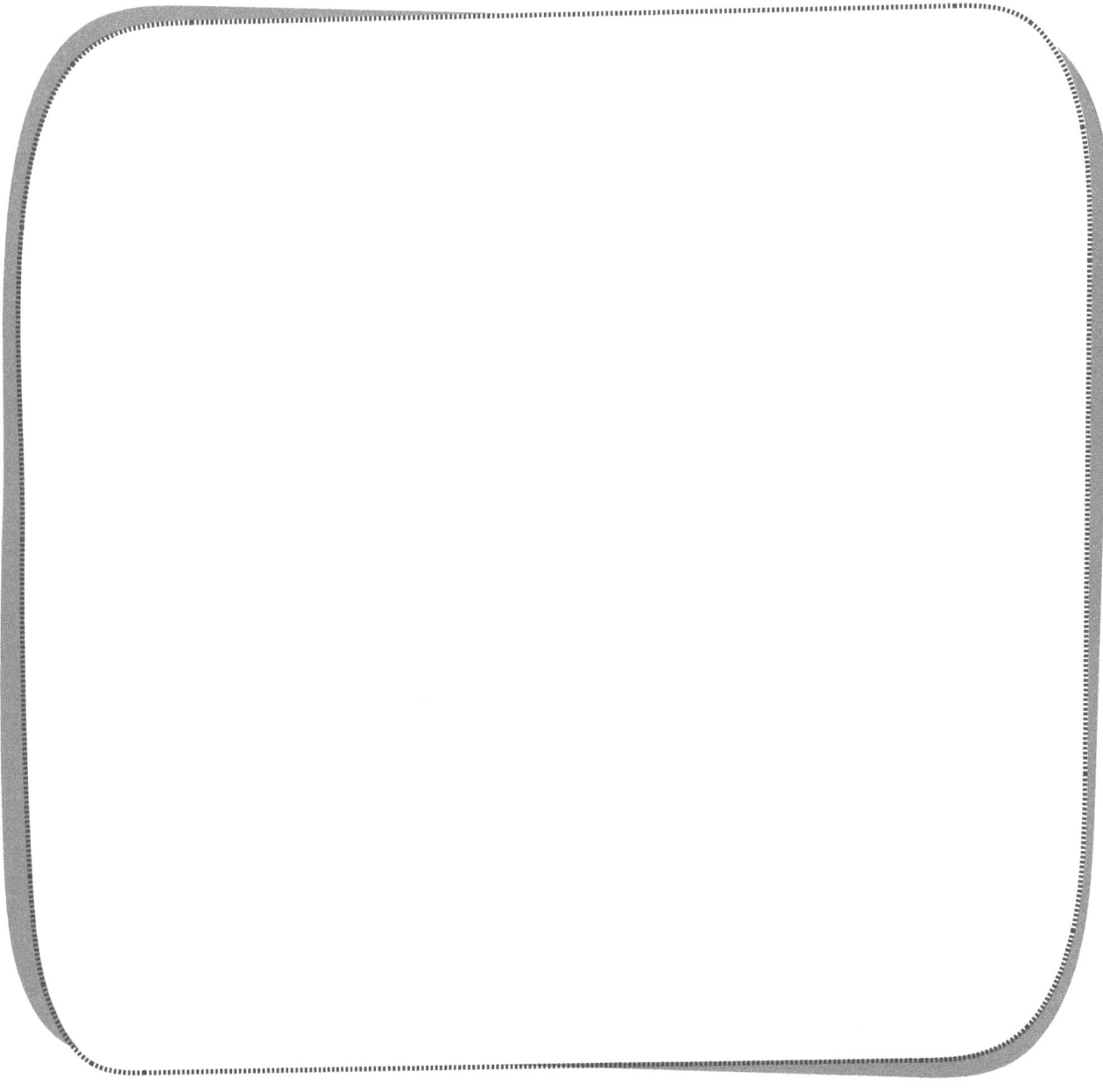

Teacher + Counselor Activity Guide

Brittle Star Arm Math

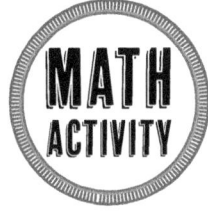

MATERIALS

- "Arm Math" worksheet
- Pencils

TEACHER INSTRUCTIONS

1. Lead a brief discussion about how brittle stars can detach or lose an arm but then regenerate or regrow a new one in its place.

2. Hand out the "Arm Math" worksheet.

3. Allow at least 20 minutes for students to complete their worksheets.

4. Review answers as a class.

 Use the blank "Arm Math" worksheet to add math problems tailored to your students' skill level.

Name: _____   Date: _____

Arm Math

DIRECTIONS: Answer each math problem and show your work by writing down all the steps you took to solve the problem.

1. Three brittle stars are playing in the ocean. They each have five arms. How many total arms are there?

2. Four brittle stars are playing a game. Two stars have five arms, and the other two stars are each missing one of their five arms. As a group, how many arms do the four stars have?

3. Betsy and Binky are playing together when a predator approaches. To escape, Betsy detaches two of her five arms. Binky, who only has four arms, detaches one arm. How many arms does Betsy now have? How many arms does Binky now have? Together, how many arms do Besty and Binky now have?

4. There are seven brittle stars sunning themselves on a reef. Four are black, and they each have five arms. Two are red, and they each have four arms. One is orange and has two arms. The black stars, together, have how many arms? The red and orange stars, together, have how many arms? If you divide the total number of black arms by the total number of red and orange arms, how many arms do you have?

5. *Bonus equation/question:*

Teacher + Counselor Activity Guide

Name: _____ **ANSWER KEY** Date: _____

Arm Math

DIRECTIONS: Answer each math problem and show your work by writing down all the steps you took to solve the problem.

1. Three brittle stars are playing in the ocean. They each have five arms. How many total arms are there?

    5 + 5 + 5 = 15 arms
    5 x 3 = 15 arms

2. Four brittle stars are playing a game. Two stars have five arms, and the other two stars are each missing one of their five arms. As a group, how many arms do the four stars have?

    5 + 5 = 10
    5 – 1 = 4
    5 – 1 = 4
    10 + 4 + 4 = 18 arms

    5 + 5 + 4 + 4 = 18 arms

    5 x 2 = 10
    4 x 2 = 8
    10 + 8 = 18 arms

3. Betsy and Binky are playing together when a predator approaches. To escape, Betsy detaches two of her five arms. Binky, who only has four arms, detaches one arm. How many arms does Betsy now have? How many arms does Binky now have? Together, how many arms do Besty and Binky now have?

    Betsy: 5 – 2 = 3 arms
    Binky: 4 – 1 = 3 arms
    Besty and Binky: 3 + 3 = 6 arms

4. There are seven brittle stars sunning themselves on a reef. Four are black, and they each have five arms. Two are red, and they each have four arms. One is orange and has two arms. The black stars, together, have how many arms? The red and orange stars, together, have how many arms? If you divide the total number of black arms by the total number of red and orange arms, how many arms do you have?

    Black stars:
    5 + 5 + 5 + 5 = 20 arms
    5 x 4 = 20 arms

    Red and Orange stars:
    Red: 4 + 4 = 8
    Orange: 2 + 0 = 2
    Total: 8 + 2 = 10 arms

    Black arms divided by Red and Orange arms:
    20 ÷ 10 = 2

5. *Bonus equation/question:*

Name: _____ Date: _____

Arm Math Bonus Questions

DIRECTIONS: Answer each math problem and show your work by writing down all the steps you took to solve the problem.

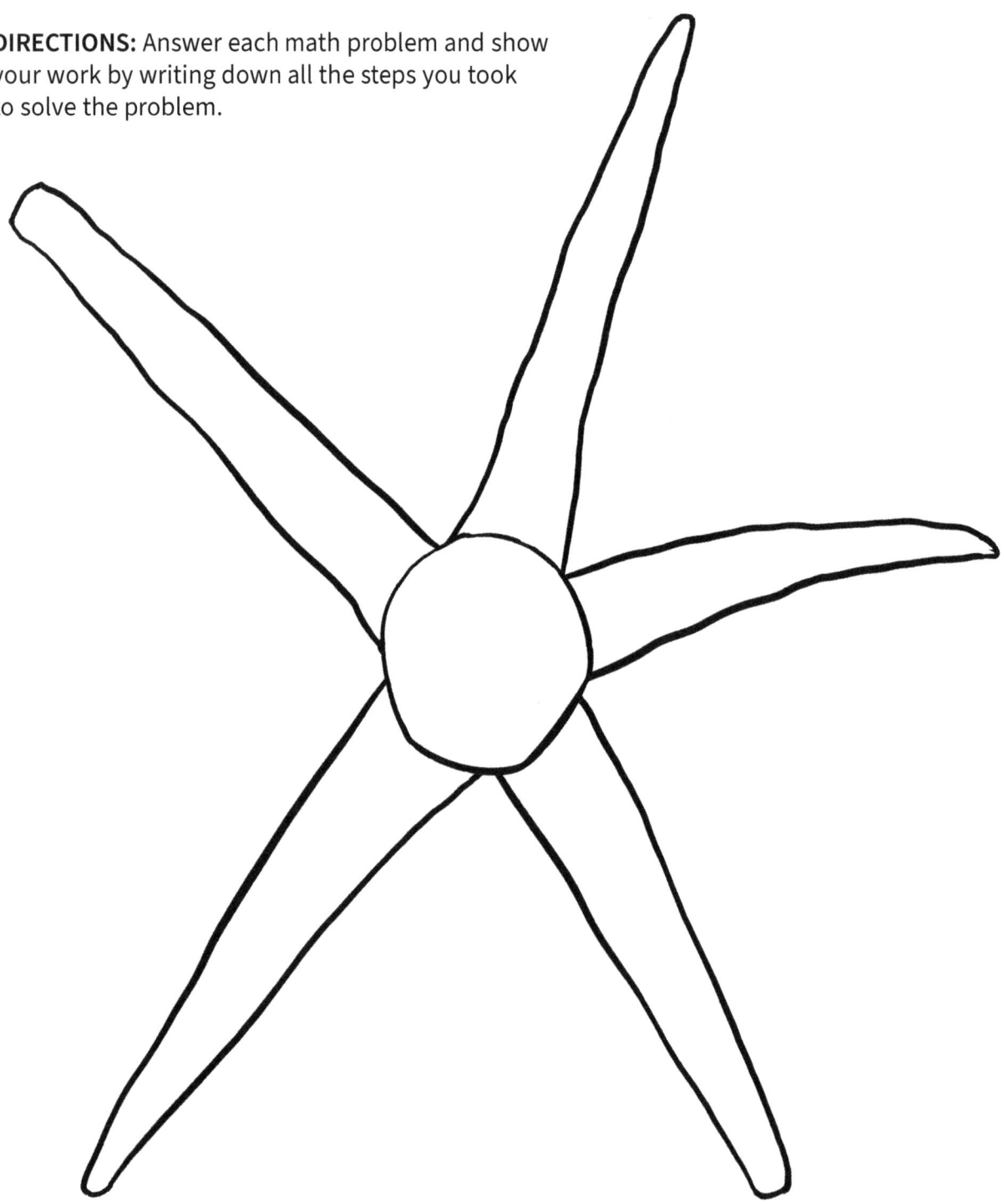

Steal the Star

MATERIALS

- Gym/Play Area
- An object to represent a brittle star (flag, ball, star squishy/plushy, stuffed animal, cone, etc.)

TEACHER INSTRUCTIONS

1. Group students into two teams.

2. Have each team stand in line on opposite sides of the gym (or play area).

3. Place the object that represents the brittle star in the center of the field of play.

4. Provide the following game rules: When the whistle blows (or you yell, "Go!"), the first runner from each team will race to the middle to capture the star. Whoever grabs the star first earns one point for their team. The second runners from each team then race to the center to capture the star. Whoever captures the star first earns two points for their team. The third runners then go, with the chance to earn three points. The fourth runners can earn four points, and so on. Continue until all team members have raced. The team with the most points at the end wins.

 For students with limited mobility or related health issues, consider modifying the game to best accommodate their needs.

DIY Instruments

MATERIALS

- Recycled materials (cardboard boxes, rubber bands, tin cans, bottlecaps, coat hangers, plastic bottles, paper plates, pipe cleaners, straws, paper towel rolls, etc.)
- Glue/Scissors/Tape/Stapler

TEACHER INSTRUCTIONS

1. Group students into teams or pairs.

2. Ask each group to create or build a musical instrument using recycled materials.

Science Activity

MATERIALS

- "Brittle Star Research Notes" worksheet
- Pencils

TEACHER INSTRUCTIONS

1. Distribute the "Brittle Star Research Notes" worksheet.

2. Instruct students to use classroom and online research tools to gather facts and information about the brittle star. Ask them to write a short essay summarizing their research findings. Encourage students to follow the outline provided on their worksheets when writing their essays.

3. Ask for volunteers to read their essays aloud.

Name: _____ Date: _____

Brittle Star Research Notes

DIRECTIONS: Use classroom resources and websites to learn facts and information about the brittle star. Write down your findings in the appropriate boxes, then use that information to write a five-paragraph essay about this invertebrate.

Paragraph 1: Introduction

Paragraph 2: Appearance

Paragraph 3: Habitat and Diet

Paragraph 4: Interesting Facts

Paragraph 5: Conclusion

Teacher + Counselor Activity Guide

Fun Facts about Brittle Stars

TECHNOLOGY ACTIVITY

MATERIALS

- "Fun Facts about Brittle Stars" worksheet
- Computer/Laptop
- Internet access

TEACHER INSTRUCTIONS

1. Pass out the "Fun Facts about Brittle Stars" worksheet.

2. Ask students to research brittle stars and answer the following questions:
    1. What can brittle stars do when they are attacked?
    2. Can brittle stars regenerate or regrow their arms?
    3. How many inches long are a brittle star's arms?
    4. How do brittle stars move?
    5. Can some brittle stars duplicate themselves?
    6. What other additional facts or interesting information did you discover?

3. Have students create a slideshow or video presentation that highlights the answers to each question and any other information students learned. Ask for volunteers to share their slideshows and videos with the class.

Name: _____   Date: _____

Fun Facts about Brittle Stars

DIRECTIONS: Research interesting facts about brittle stars and then answer the questions below. Use the answers and any other information you learn to create a slideshow or video presentation.

1. What can brittle stars do when they are attacked? _____
   _____
   _____

2. Can brittle stars regenerate or regrow their arms? _____
   _____
   _____

3. How many inches long are a brittle star's arms? _____
   _____
   _____

4. How do brittle stars move? _____
   _____
   _____

5. Can some brittle stars duplicate themselves? _____
   _____
   _____

6. What other additional facts or interesting information did you discover? _____
   _____
   _____
   _____
   _____

Writing Activities

MATERIALS

- "Vocabulary Words" worksheet
- "Describe the Picture" worksheet
- "Finish the Sentence" worksheet
- "Do You Prefer Working by Yourself or with a Team?" worksheet
- "Teamwork or No Teamwork" worksheet
- Pencils

TEACHER INSTRUCTIONS

1. Pass out all five worksheets for students to complete at one time, or have them complete one worksheet per day during the school week.

2. Instruct students to fill out their worksheets and be prepared to discuss their answers as a group.

3. Allow enough time for students to complete the writing activity, then review and discuss the assignment as a group.

Name: _____ Date: _____

Vocabulary Words

DIRECTIONS: Write original sentences that include the vocabulary words listed below. Each word needs to be used at least once, and a sentence can have more than one vocabulary word in it. When all the words have been used in sentences, draw a comic strip or a picture that represents or reflects as many of the vocabulary words as possible.

Vocabulary Words: Team, Work, Together, Combine, Achieve, Sharing, Caring, Listen, Idea, Compromise

Teacher + Counselor Activity Guide

Name: _____ Date: _____

Describe the Picture

DIRECTIONS: Look at the picture and then fill in the worksheet.

1. This is a picture of what? _____
_____

2. What is happening in the picture? _____
_____
_____

3. Where do you think this picture was taken (setting/location)? _____
_____
_____

4. Write an original sentence that includes your answers to the questions above: _____
_____
_____
_____
_____
_____
_____
_____
_____
_____
_____
_____
_____
_____

99

Name: _____   Date: _____

Finish the Sentence

DIRECTIONS: Complete the sentence and then draw a picture to match your sentence.

I WILL BE A GOOD TEAMMATE BY _____

_____
_____
_____
_____
_____

Teacher + Counselor Activity Guide

Name: _____ Date: _____

Do You Prefer Working by Yourself or with a Team?

DIRECTIONS: Fill in the worksheet by answering if you prefer to work "by yourself" or "with a team." Write down three reasons to support your answer.

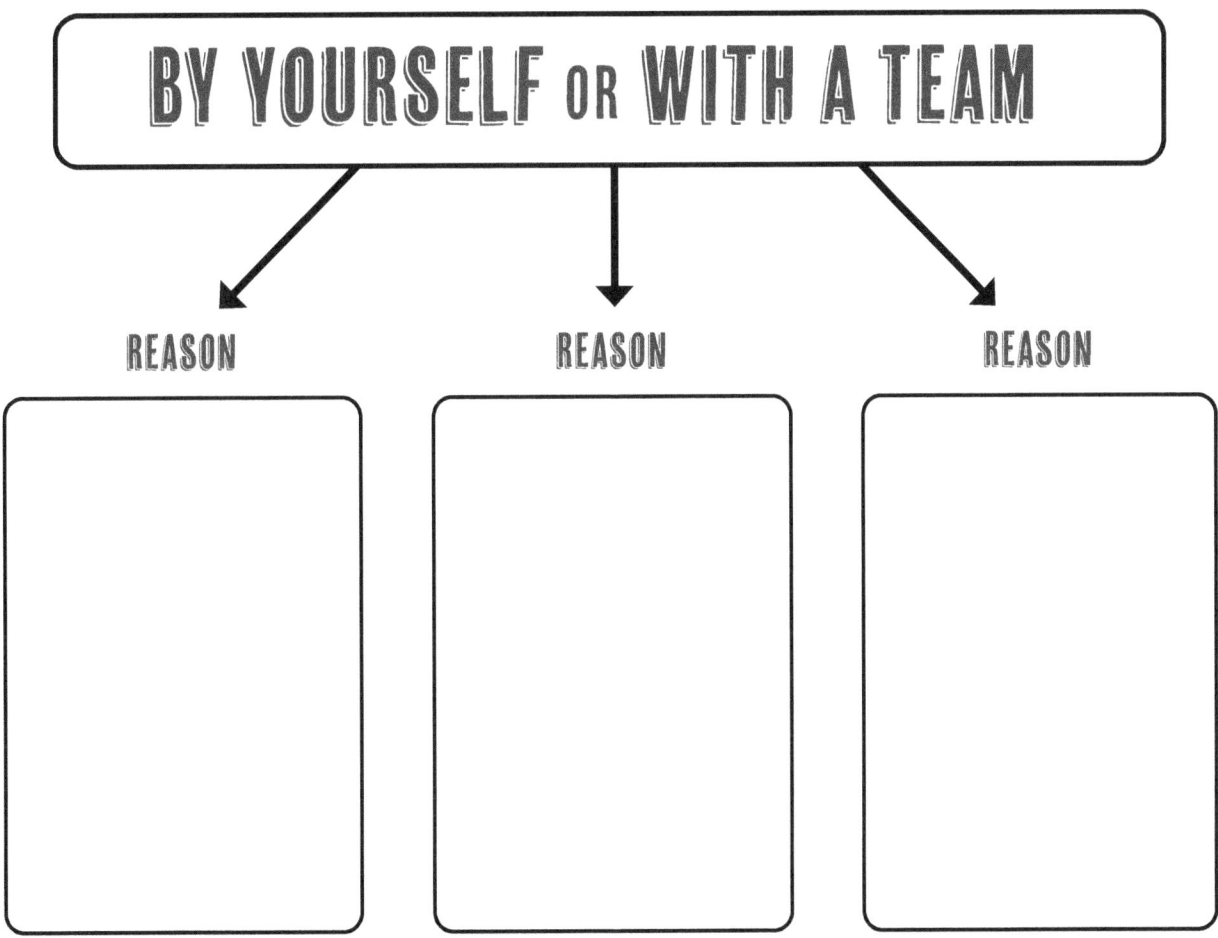

Name: _____ Date: _____

Teamwork or No Teamwork

DIRECTIONS: Read the text and then answer the questions.

TEXT: Think about a situation where you were on a team (or in a group) and everyone worked together. Then think about a situation where you were on a team (or in a group) and no one worked together. Situations can involve class projects, sports teams, school government, etc.

1. Describe a situation where you were on a team (or in a group) and everyone worked together: _____
   _____
   _____

2. What did it feel like to be on that team or in that group? _____
   _____
   _____
   _____

3. Describe a situation where you were on a team (or in a group) and no one worked together: _____
   _____
   _____
   _____

4. What did it feel like to be on that team or in that group? _____
   _____
   _____
   _____
   _____

DISCO CLAM

SKILL

KACIE, A DISCO CLAM, IS A "CLASS CLOWN." SHE LOVES TO JOKE AROUND AND HAVE A GOOD TIME. SHE LIKES TO TEASE HER FRIENDS. EVEN THOUGH SHE'S A JOKESTER, SHE UNDERSTANDS THE IMPORTANCE OF SELF-CONTROL AND ONLY USING NICE TEASES. KACIE TEACHES US THE IMPORTANCE OF HAVING SELF-CONTROL AND USING NICE TEASES INSTEAD OF MEAN TEASES.

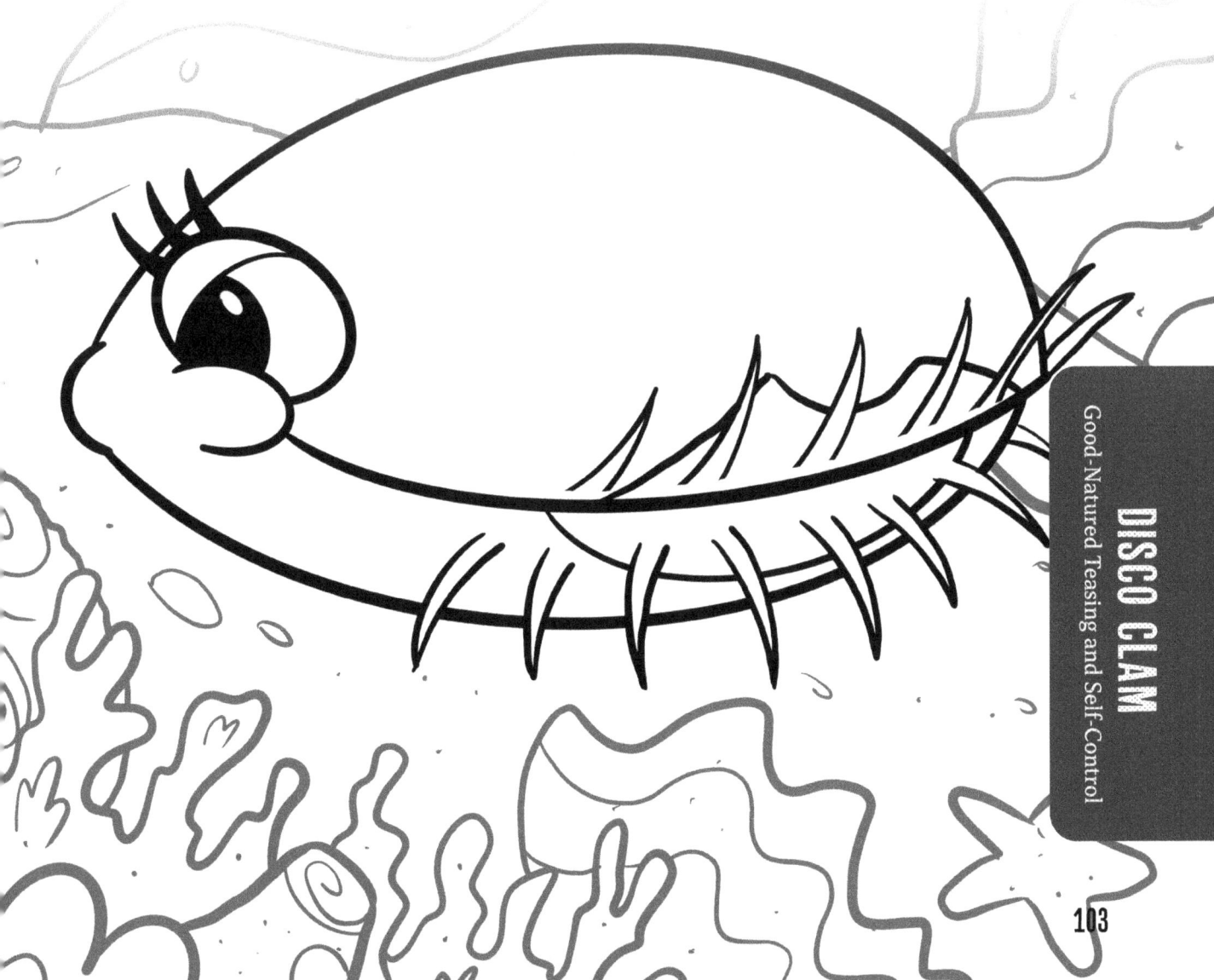

DISCO CLAM — Good-Natured Teasing and Self-Control

The name Kacie means alert and watchful.

Kacie Clam likes to act like a clown.
She loves to have fun and joke around.

While Kacie would love to joke around the whole entire day,
she knows there are limits if she wants her friends to stay.

Kacie Clam knows she can only tease when her peers are on board.
All need to be equally partaking, with nothing said or done that's untoward.

This is called a nice tease, when all involved are having fun.
If they are not having fun, then the jokes need to be done.

If someone feels hurt, it is no longer okay.
No one involved in a joke should ever be made to feel gray.

A mean tease is when you intentionally disconcert.
A joke should never lead to anyone feeling this hurt.

Teacher + Counselor Activity Guide

Q: When a disco clam spews toxic mucus, it is doing this: eating/talking to other clams/letting go of anger/protecting itself

A: Protecting Itself

*Kacie would never hurt her friends intentionally.
She only uses teases conventionally.*

*While it's fun to joke all day,
there are limits to her play.*

*Kacie never wants to get out of control,
especially when she's on a really long teasing roll.*

*Sometimes Kacie Clam uses her inner speech,
and tells herself to take a break on the beach.*

*She slowly breathes in and out,
until she feels calm throughout.*

*Once she feels serene,
she goes back to reconvene.*

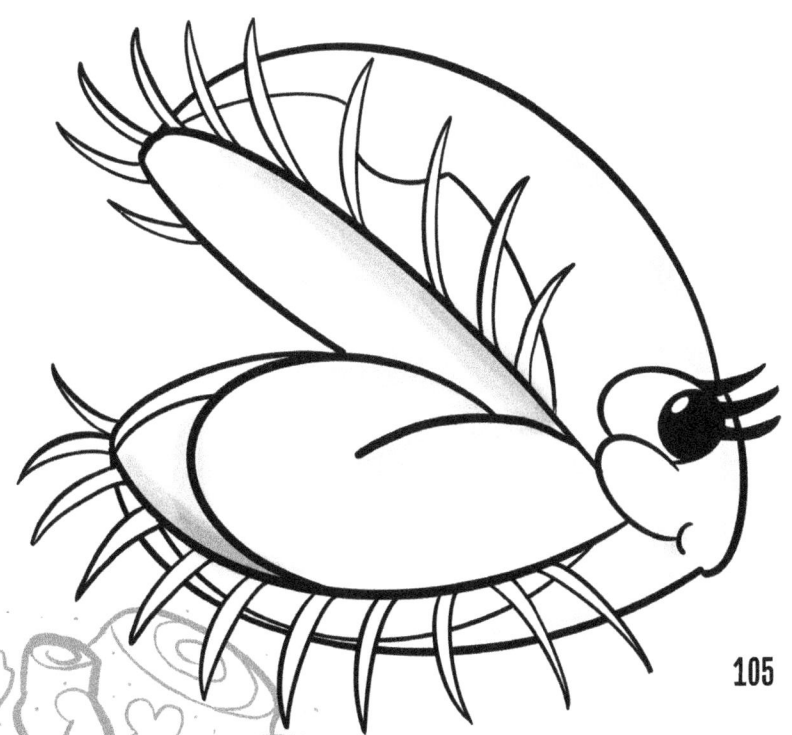

Paper Plate Clam

MATERIALS

- Paper plates
- Colored Pencils/Crayons/Markers
- Googly eyes
- Glue

TEACHER INSTRUCTIONS

1. Pass out paper plates to each student.

2. Have students fold their plates in half, to represent the disco clam, and then ask them to color their clams and attach googly eyes. Eyes can be drawn on, if googly eyes are unavailable.

3. Group students into teams after they finish designing their clams.

4. Instruct the groups to create their own role-play scenarios that demonstrate the differences between nice teasing and mean teasing.

5. Share examples if groups have trouble developing ideas. (A friend trips going up the stairs and drops her books; A classmate has a stain on his shirt; Someone drops their tray in the cafeteria, etc.)

6. Have groups perform their role-plays for the whole class and then lead a discussion about the differences between nice teasing and mean teasing.

 You may want to review each group's role-play scenario before they perform to ensure it is appropriate.

Teacher + Counselor Activity Guide

Kacie Disco Clam Discussion Questions

MATERIALS

- Pencils
- "Discussion Questions" worksheet

TEACHER INSTRUCTIONS

1. Pass out the "Discussion Questions" worksheet.
2. Instruct students to fill out the worksheet by answering the questions.
3. Read the questions aloud and discuss possible answers as a group.

CLASS/GROUP DISCUSSION QUESTIONS

1. What is nice teasing?
2. Why is it important for everyone to feel comfortable when joking around or teasing?
3. What is mean teasing?
4. If your teasing hurts someone's feelings, what should you do?
5. What is one thing you can do to calm down or relax when you need a break?

Name: _____ Date: _____

Discussion Questions

DIRECTIONS: In the space provided, answer the following questions. Be prepared to discuss your answers with the group.

1. What is nice teasing? _____
   _____
   _____

2. Why is it important for everyone to feel comfortable when joking around or teasing? ___
   _____
   _____

3. What is mean teasing? _____
   _____
   _____

4. If your teasing hurts someone's feelings, what should you do?_____
   _____
   _____
   _____

5. What is one thing you can do to calm down or relax when you need a break? _____
   _____
   _____
   _____

Teacher + Counselor Activity Guide

Drawing Activity

MATERIALS

- Colored Pencils/Crayons/Markers
- "Nice Teasing vs. Mean Teasing" Paper/Poster Board

TEACHER INSTRUCTIONS

1. Distribute the "Nice Teasing vs. Mean Teasing" paper/poster board.

2. Review with students the directions for the poster.

3. Ask for volunteers to show and explain their drawings.

Name: _____ Date: _____

Nice Teasing vs. Mean Teasing Poster

DIRECTIONS: Draw a comic strip or picture that shows the differences between nice teasing and mean teasing. Include words and dialogue.

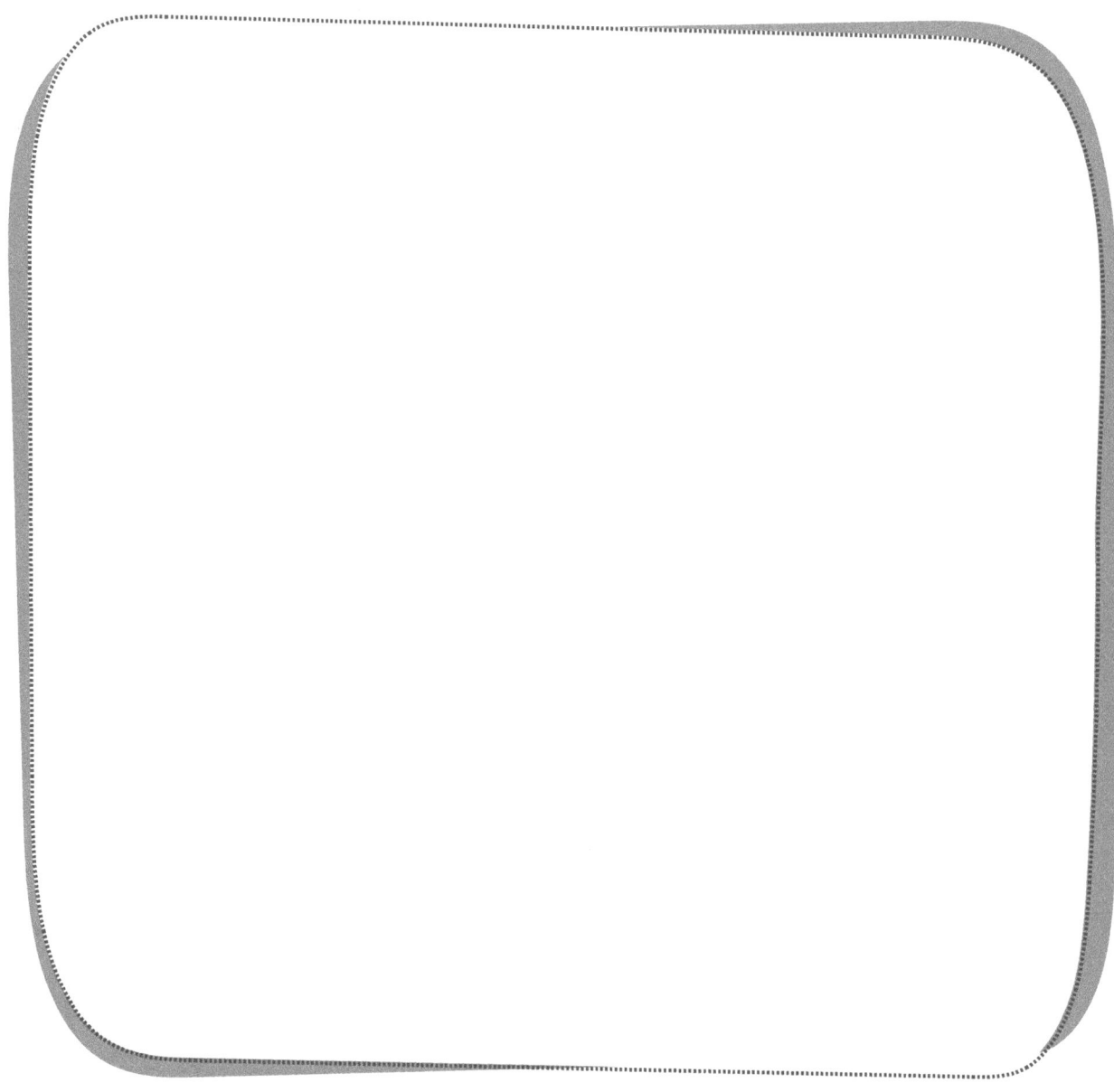

Teacher + Counselor Activity Guide

Clam Roll Bowling

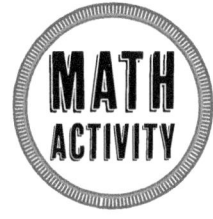

MATERIALS

- Gym/Play Area
- Two sets of ten plastic bottles (one set per team)
- Two rubber balls
- Pencils
- Lined paper
- Clipboards

TEACHER INSTRUCTIONS

1. Number the plastic bottles in each set 1 through 10, then stand the first set of bottles in a triangle formation like bowling pins. Stand the second set of bottles in a similar formation several feet away.

2. Group students into two bowling teams.

3. Have each team stand 50 to 60 feet away from the pins. Give each team a rubber ball and instruct one member from each team to roll the ball (which represents the clam) at their designated pins. The goal is to knock down as many pins as possible. After they roll, have them record on their paper the number of pins they knocked down. Then instruct them to reset the pins for the next team member. When every team member has had a chance to roll the "clam," have teams tally the total number of pins their team members knocked down. The team with the highest number wins.

OPTIONAL Customize the game by giving each pin a value and having students add the value of the pins they knocked down rather than the number of pins. You also can incorporate other math problems by having the teams multiply, divide, or subtract their two scores.

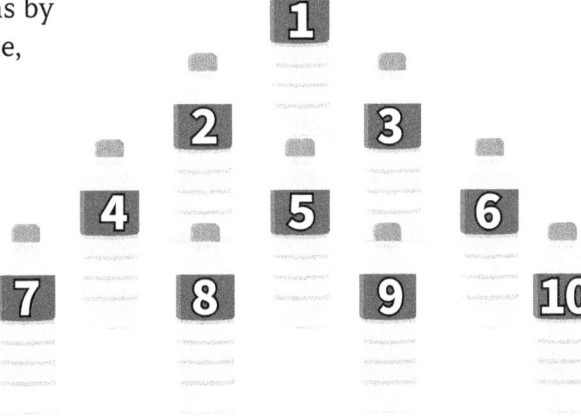

111

Hurl the Clams

MATERIALS

- Gym/Play Area
- Badminton net
- Badminton rackets
- Bean bags
- Hula hoops

TEACHER INSTRUCTIONS

1. Erect a badminton net (or other similar divider).

2. Place three to five hula hoops on the ground on one side of the net.

3. Have three to five students (players) stand on the opposite side of the net. Give each player a badminton racket and five bean bags (representing clams).

4. Assign each player a specific hula hoop and instruct them to toss each bean bag (or clam) over the net and into their designated hula hoop. The player who gets the most clams inside their hula hoop wins the round. The next group of three to five players then go, and so on until everyone has participated. The winners of each round can then play each other in a "championship" final round.

 For students with limited mobility or related health issues, consider modifying the game to best accommodate their needs.

Self-Control Musical Statues

MATERIALS

- Music Player
- Gym/Play Area

TEACHER INSTRUCTIONS

1. Instruct students to move and/or dance around when the music begins. When the music stops, they need to freeze in place like a statue and remain frozen for at least 10 seconds. Any student who cannot maintain their pose for 10 seconds is out of the game.

2. Continue playing the game by extending the length of time students must freeze like a statue. For example, start with 10 seconds in the first round, 20 seconds in the second round, 30 seconds in the third round, and so on until there is a winner.

Science Activity

MATERIALS

- "Disco Clam Research Notes" worksheet
- Pencils

TEACHER INSTRUCTIONS

1. Distribute the "Disco Clam Research Notes" worksheet.

2. Instruct students to use classroom and online research tools to gather facts and information about the disco clam. Ask them to write a short essay summarizing their research findings. Encourage students to follow the outline provided on their worksheets when writing their essays.

3. Ask for volunteers to read their essays aloud.

Teacher + Counselor Activity Guide

Name: _____ Date: _____

Disco Clam Research Notes

DIRECTIONS: Use classroom resources and websites to learn facts and information about the disco clam. Write down your findings in the appropriate boxes, then use that information to write a five-paragraph essay about this mollusk.

Paragraph 1: Introduction

Paragraph 2: Appearance

Paragraph 3: Habitat and Diet

Paragraph 4: Interesting Facts

Paragraph 5: Conclusion

Fun Facts about Disco Clams

MATERIALS

- "Fun Facts about Disco Clams" worksheet
- Computer/Laptop
- Internet access

TEACHER INSTRUCTIONS

1. Pass out the "Fun Facts about Disco Clams" worksheet.

2. Ask students to research disco clams and answer the following questions:

    1. How big is a typical disco clam?
    2. When born, all disco clams are what gender?
    3. How many eyes do disco clams have?
    4. How do disco clams produce flashing "lights"?
    5. Why do you think disco clams create or use flashing lights?
    6. What other additional facts or interesting information did you discover?

3. Have students create a slideshow or video presentation that highlights the answers to each question and any other information students learned. Ask for volunteers to share their slideshows and videos with the class.

Name: _____   Date: _____

Fun Facts about Disco Clams

DIRECTIONS: Research interesting facts about disco clams and then answer the questions below. Use the answers and any other information you learn to create a slideshow or video presentation.

1. How big is a typical disco clam? _____
   _____
   _____

2. When born, all disco clams are what gender?_____
   _____
   _____

3. How many eyes do disco clams have?_____
   _____
   _____

4. How do disco clams produce flashing "lights"? _____
   _____
   _____

5. Why do you think disco clams create or use flashing lights? _____
   _____
   _____

6. What other additional facts or interesting information did you discover? ____
   _____
   _____

Writing Activities

MATERIALS

- "Vocabulary Words" worksheet
- "Describe the Picture" worksheet
- "Finish the Sentence" worksheet
- "Do You Think It Is Okay to Tease a Friend?" worksheet
- "A Teasing Situation" worksheet
- Pencils

TEACHER INSTRUCTIONS

1. Pass out all five worksheets for students to complete at one time, or have them complete one worksheet per day during the school week.

2. Instruct students to fill out their worksheets and be prepared to discuss their answers as a group.

3. Allow enough time for students to complete the writing activity, then review and discuss the assignment as a group.

Name: _____ Date: _____

Vocabulary Words

DIRECTIONS: Write original sentences that include the vocabulary words listed below. Each word needs to be used at least once, and a sentence can have more than one vocabulary word in it. When all the words have been used in sentences, draw a comic strip or a picture that represents or reflects as many of the vocabulary words as possible.

Vocabulary Words: Joke, Tease, Equally, Nice, Agrees, Fun, Feels, Hurt, Mean, Friends

_____
_____
_____
_____
_____
_____
_____
_____
_____
_____
_____
_____
_____
_____
_____
_____

Under the Sea Lessons for Life – Volume 2

Name: _____ Date: _____

Describe the Picture

DIRECTIONS: Look at the picture and then fill in the worksheet.

1. This is a picture of what? _____
   _____

2. What is happening in the picture? _____
   _____
   _____

3. Where do you think this picture was taken (setting/location)? _____
   _____
   _____

4. Write an original sentence that includes your answers to the questions above: _____
   _____
   _____
   _____

Name: _____ Date: _____

Finish the Sentence

DIRECTIONS: Complete the sentence and then draw a picture to match your sentence.

THE DIFFERENCE BETWEEN A NICE TEASE AND A MEAN TEASE IS_____
_____
_____
_____
_____
_____

Name: _____ Date: _____

Do You Think It Is Okay to Tease a Friend?

DIRECTIONS: Fill in the worksheet by answering yes or no if you think it is okay to tease a friend. Write down three reasons to support your answer.

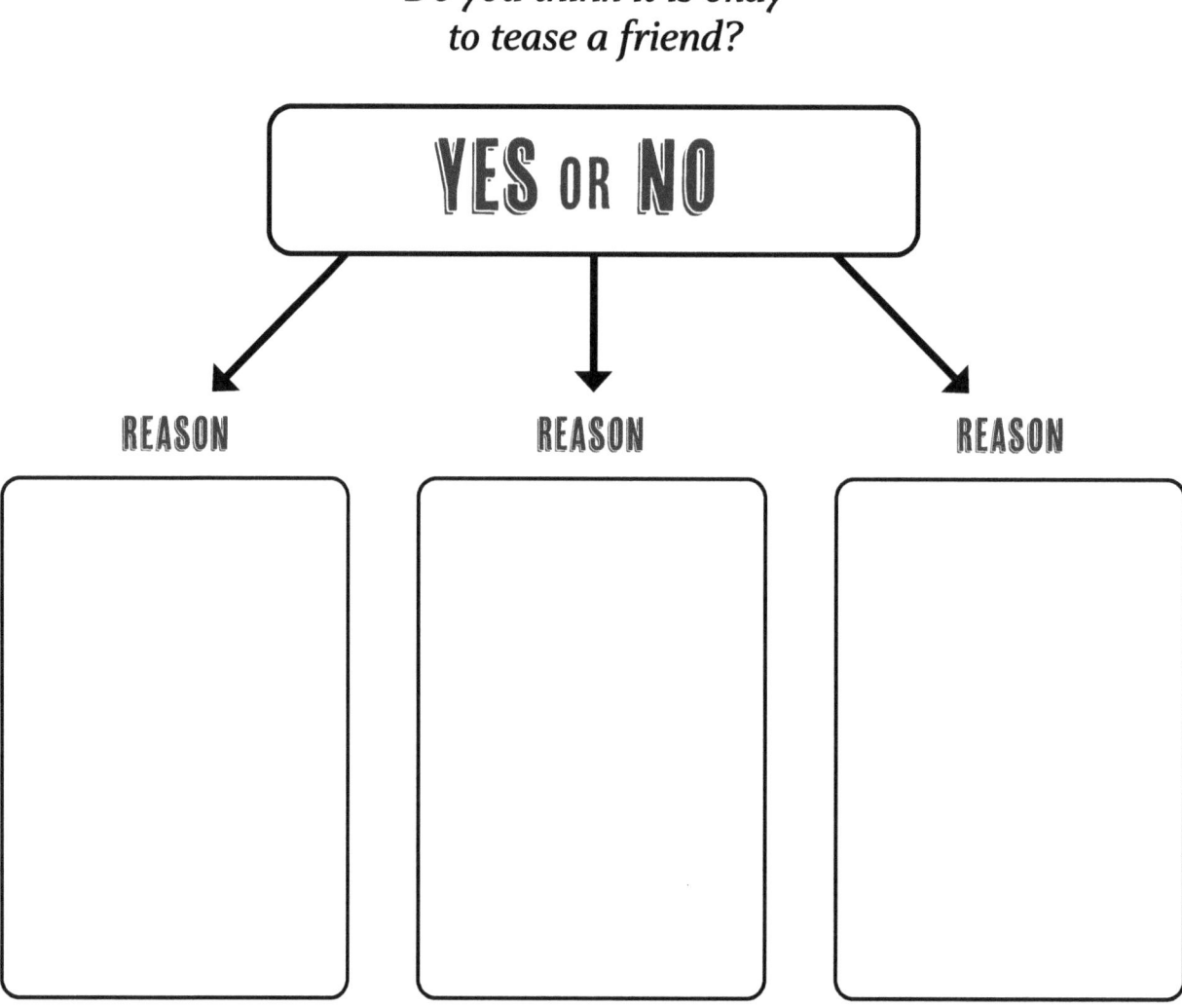

Name: _____ Date: _____

A Teasing Situation

DIRECTIONS: Read the text and then answer the questions.

TEXT: Think about a situation where someone teased you.

1. Describe the teasing situation: _____
   _____

2. Was it nice teasing or mean teasing? _____
   _____
   _____

3. If it was nice teasing, how did it make you feel? If it was mean teasing, how did it make you feel? _____
   _____
   _____

4. How did you react to the teasing? Would you react the same way if it happened again? If yes, why? If no, why not? _____
   _____
   _____
   _____
   _____
   _____

NOTES

Teacher + Counselor Activity Guide

ANSWER KEYS

MANDARIN FISH / TECHNOLOGY ACTIVITY

Physical Appearance of the Mandarin Fish

Page 19

1. Do Mandarin fish have scales?
   No

2. What covers the body of the Mandarin fish?
   A smelly, mucus coating

3. How do the vibrant colors of the Mandarin fish help them?
   Serves as a warning to predators that they are toxic

4. How do the females and males differ in appearance?
   Males are larger, with a longer dorsal fin

5. What is the average length of a Mandarin fish?
   Three inches

REFERENCES:
https://oceanblueproject.org/the-beautiful-mandarin-fish/
https://ocean.si.edu/ocean-life/fish/mandarinfish-duo
https://www.onekindplanet.org/animal/mandarin-fish/

EPAULETTE SHARK / TECHNOLOGY ACTIVITY

The Walking Shark

Page 46

1. How do epaulette sharks walk?
   Using their pelvic and pectoral fins

2. What can an epaulette shark do to conserve energy?
   Switch off parts of its brain

3. Where do epaulette sharks typically walk?
   Sea floor; Reef structures; Between shallow tidal pools

4. Do epaulette sharks also swim?
   Yes

5. How long can an epaulette shark go without oxygen?
   1 hour (without adverse effects)

REFERENCES:
https://ocean.si.edu/ocean-life/sharks-rays/epaulette-shark
https://www.neaq.org/animal/epaulette-shark/
https://www.oceanicsociety.org/resources/ocean-facts/the-shark-that-can-walk-on-land/
https://www.aquariumofpacific.org/onlinelearningcenter/species/epaulette_shark1/

ANSWER KEYS

NUDIBRANCH / TECHNOLOGY ACTIVITY

Fun Facts about Nudibranchs

Page 69

1. What type of animal is the nudibranch?
   Mollusk

2. What makes the nudibranch unique?
   Regrows or regenerates body parts

3. How long do nudibranchs live?
   Up to a year

4. How do nudibranchs communicate with each other?
   Chemical signals in the slime trail they leave

5. What is unique about the appearance of their eggs?
   Typically laid in a spiral or ribbon-like formation

REFERENCES:

https://www.pacificbeachcoalition.org/nudibranchs-fun-facts/

https://kids.nationalgeographic.com/animals/invertebrates/facts/nudibranch

https://greatsouthernreef.com/nudibranch

https://www.oceandimensions.com/how-do-nudibranchs-find-each-other-in-the-big-wide-open-ocean/

BRITTLE STAR / TECHNOLOGY ACTIVITY

Fun Facts about Brittle Stars

Page 96

1. What can brittle stars do when they are attacked?
   Detach one or more arms to escape

2. Can brittle stars regenerate or regrow their arms?
   Yes

3. How many inches long are a brittle star's arms?
   About 24 inches

4. How do brittle stars move?
   By twisting and bending their arms

5. Can some brittle stars duplicate themselves?
   Yes, in a process called asexual reproduction

REFERENCES:

https://ocean.si.edu/ocean-life/invertebrates/brittle-star-splits#

https://www.montereybayaquarium.org/animals/animals-a-to-z/deep-sea-brittle-star

https://oceanconservancy.org/blog/2019/08/13/difference-sea-brittle-stars/

Teacher + Counselor Activity Guide

ANSWER KEYS

DISCO CLAM / TECHNOLOGY ACTIVITY

Fun Facts about Disco Clams

Page 117

1. How big is a typical disco clam?

   Up to 4 inches long, but most are between 1 and 3 inches long

2. When born, all disco clams are what gender?

   Male; As they age, they turn female

3. How many eyes do disco clams have?

   Around 40

4. How do disco clams produce flashing "lights"?

   Reflective spheres on one of its lips catches light and reflects it outward, then its other lip catches and absorbs that reflected light, creating a flashing effect.

5. Why do you think disco clams use flashing lights?

   Deter predators; Attract a mate

REFERENCES:
https://www.livescience.com/49312-why-disco-clams-flash.html
https://a-z-animals.com/animals/disco-clam/
https://www.colorado.edu/cumuseum/2021/01/06/disco-clams

TIPS TO SHARE WITH PARENTS

Encourage parents to support and reinforce the messages and lessons of each story at home by sharing with them these handy and timely tips:

FRODO MANDARIN FISH
Self-Confidence, Diversity, and Acceptance

- Teach kids how they can report bullying or other hurtful behaviors, who the trusted adults are at school and in their neighborhood that they can reach out to, and how to keep themselves safe.
- Role-play situations that allow kids to practice and become more confident standing up for themselves when someone is being mean.
- Encourage kids to practice saying I-statements to express their feelings, and then using I-statements to let others know how they feel. (You can learn more about I-statements by reading about Ollie Octopus in Volume 1 of *Under the Sea: Lessons for Life*.)
- Remind kids it is okay to be different. Help them embrace what makes them unique and teach them to be accepting of other people's differences.

SHAKTI EPAULETTE SHARK
Assertiveness and Accountability

- When kids are dealing with challenging situations, support them by offering guidance on what they can do to make the situation better. Ask questions to help them see and understand what they have the power to control and what things about a situation are not in their control.
- Define what it means to be a trusted adult and ask your kids to identify three individuals they can go to for help when they are at home, in school, or in the community.
- Discuss the differences between bullying (repeated behaviors, power/control imbalances, and unwanted or aggressive behaviors) and a mean moment (single event, done without thinking, etc.).
- Role-play different ways your kids can report bullying behaviors to a trusted adult.

Teacher + Counselor Activity Guide

TIPS

NIKO NUDIBRANCH
Problem Solving and Bullying

- Model problem solving by including kids in your own decision-making process.
- Brainstorm possible options for dealing with problems, including the pros and cons of each option.
- Give kids the space to struggle with and work through their decisions and learn from their mistakes.
- Ask your kids to name the special skills or talents they have, and encourage them to embrace those skills and talents.
- Teach kids they have the power to say, "No!" and role-play different ways they can say, "No" when someone pressures them to do something that is harmful or mean.
- Explain the differences between reporting someone's behavior (trying to keep someone out of trouble) and tattling (trying to get someone into trouble).

SEABORN BRITTLE STAR
Compromising and Teamwork

- Be a role model. Kids are always watching how adults react to events and situations, and they will learn and adopt similar behaviors. Demonstrate how to compromise and cooperate so your kids can see and hear what that looks and sounds like. For example, if someone expresses an opposing opinion, model an appropriate response by acknowledging their perspective and respectfully expressing yours.
- Talk about the value and importance of compromising with friends, family, and others. Use examples from your family's life or events in the community as teaching opportunities to show how one's willingness to compromise can help foster respect, build trust, and lead to greater understanding.
- Teach your children to celebrate, recognize, and respect the strengths and talents of others. In group activities, whether it's sports or music, when everyone feels welcome, contributes, and works together, the results are often more rewarding and successful.

KACIE DISCO CLAM
Good-Natured Teasing and Self-Control

- Have conversations about what nice teasing looks and sounds like, and when teasing can cross the line (laughing at someone, not with them; teasing someone after being told to stop; teasing that tries to hurt or humiliate someone, etc.).

- Use role-play to practice with your children how to use I-statements when their feelings get hurt by someone whose jokes and teases are mean-spirited.

- Remind your kids that they have strengths and weaknesses, just like everyone else. The more awareness they have of their weaknesses, the less likely they are to be critical of others' limitations.

- Ask if they have ever been hurt because someone joked about or teased them, then talk about what they can say to stand up for themselves and be assertive, without being mean or aggressive.

Teacher + Counselor Activity Guide

GLOSSARY

Frodo Mandarin Fish
Enlightened: to have knowledge and awareness; to be educated
Threatened: made to feel unsafe or scared; bullied
Insecure: to lack confidence; to be worried about something
Appreciation: to admire; to know something is valuable or important

Shakti Epaulette Shark
Harassed: made to feel uncomfortable or unsafe; bullied
Hilarious: funny; amusing
Commotions: disorder; unrest

Niko Nudibranch
Versatility: to have many skills; talented
Threatened: made to feel unsafe or scared; bullied
Intervene: to get involved in a situation
Accidentally: not on purpose; mistake
Crucial: important; vital
Undeterred: to show determination; to be persistent

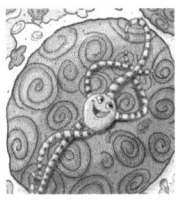
Seaborn Brittle Star
Flexible: able to change or adapt
Slithering: to move in a twisting motion
Appreciating: to like or value something
Compromise: to give and take; to reach agreement

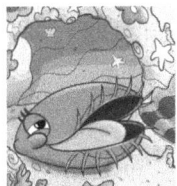
Kacie Disco Clam
Partaking: to join in
Untoward: to be inappropriate
Disconcert: to cause confusion or disorder
Intentionally: to do on purpose; planned
Conventionally: to do something in a typical, accepted, or traditional way
Serene: calm; peaceful
Reconvene: to gather together again after a pause, or to come back together again

www.ingramcontent.com/pod-product-compliance
Lightning Source LLC
LaVergne TN
LVHW070522070526
838199LV00072B/6678